Gollancz Endangered Animals Encyclopaedia for Children

Giant panda

Previous page: Resplendent quetzal
Facing page: Hochstetter's frog

Gollancz Endangered Animals Encyclopaedia for Children

ROGER FEW

Victor Gollancz
London

A Marshall Edition
This book was conceived, edited and designed by
Marshall Editions
170 Piccadilly, London W1V 9DD

Copyright © Marshall Editions Developments
Limited 1993

Foreword © 1993 by Laurence Pringle

First published in Great Britain 1993
by Victor Gollancz
an imprint of Cassell
Villiers House, 41/47 Strand, London WC2N 5JE

A catalogue record for this book is
available from the British Library

All rights reserved. No part of this book may be
reproduced or transmitted in any form or by any
means, electronic or mechanical, including
photocopying, recording, or by any information
storage and retrieval systems, without permission
in writing from the Publisher.

ISBN 0 575 05565 0

Editor: Jinny Johnson
Art editor: Eddie Poulton
Research: Jazz Wilson
Picture research: Elizabeth Loving

Film supplied by Dorchester Typesetting Group, UK
Origination by Chroma Graphics, Singapore
Printed and bound in Italy by New Interlitho SpA, Milan

CONTENTS

- 6 Foreword
- 8 Wildlife under threat
- 10 Counting the cost
- 12 Saving species
- 14 Saving habitats

16 NORTH AMERICA AND THE CARIBBEAN
- 18 Threatened animals of North America and the Caribbean
- 20 Forest and woodland animals
- 22 Focus on: Kemp's ridley turtle
- 24 Grassland and desert animals
- 26 Freshwater and sea animals

28 SOUTH AMERICA
- 30 South America's threatened animals
- 32 Rainforest animals
- 34 Focus on: Hyacinth macaw
- 36 Grassland and mountain animals
- 38 Freshwater animals

40 AFRICA
- 42 Africa's threatened animals
- 44 Rainforest animals
- 46 Focus on: African elephant
- 48 Grassland and desert animals
- 50 Freshwater and sea animals

52 EUROPE
54 Europe's threatened animals
56 Grassland and woodland animals
58 Focus on: European otter
60 Freshwater and sea animals

62 ASIA
64 Asia's threatened animals
66 Rainforest animals
68 Focus on: Orangutan
70 Grassland and mountain animals
72 Freshwater and sea animals

74 AUSTRALIA AND NEW ZEALAND
76 Threatened animals of Australia and New Zealand
78 Forest animals
80 Focus on: Dugong
82 Grassland and scrubland animals

84 OCEANIC ISLANDS
86 Threatened animals of Oceanic Islands
88 Forest animals
90 Focus on: Hawaiian goose
92 Scrubland and coastal animals

94 Resource list
95 Index
96 Acknowledgements

Bridled nail-tail wallaby

FOREWORD

Earth, our home, is a strange and wonderful place. Its neighbouring planets are utterly lifeless, but earth's atmosphere makes it an oasis in space. It is rich in habitats, from coral reefs to mountain peaks, that are living places for an incredible variety of plants and animals.

Dalmatian pelican

Scientists are amazed by the diversity of life on earth. More than 1.5 million kinds, or species, of living things have been named so far. Although most species of mammals, birds and fishes are known, millions of species of insects and other small creatures await discovery. Some scientists believe that earth may be home to 30 million species of insects alone.

Whatever the total number of species, we know very little about most life on earth. We have learned a lot about certain animals and the plants that we use for food, but little about all the other living organisms. Their lives are mysteries, as are their links with other living things, their roles in nature, and their possible value to humans.

It would be tragic to destroy so much of earth's life before it has been discovered and studied, but that is what people are doing. We are causing a rapid and massive loss of earth's great wealth of plants and animals, mostly through changing or destroying wild habitats.

This detailed guide explains why extinctions are occurring, and what people can do to save species in danger. It explores forests, deserts, and other habitats in earth's seven geographical regions. For each region, a special "Focus" feature looks more closely at an endangered species and efforts to save it.

A variety of endangered animals from each habitat are described and illustrated in colour. They include the well-known African elephant and whooping crane, but also salamanders, curlews, ghost bats and many other less familiar creatures.

Most endangered species are not well known. Many are not attractive or appealing to humans. Some, such as bats, are disliked and misunderstood by many people. Nevertheless, these creatures often play vital roles in nature. They are all part of the only life known to exist in the universe, and worth a great effort to keep alive in the wild habitats of this home we share.

Laurence Pringle

American alligator

Wildlife under threat

Animals of all kinds have been struggling to survive as our world changes. Day by day people require ever more space, more food, more water, more belongings, more fuel and more roads. All these demands put a squeeze on the earth's resources, including its wildlife.

The biggest problem for wildlife today is that, as people destroy and change natural landscapes, animals lose the places they need to live in, to find food and shelter. Wildlife habitats disappear to make way for farms, roads, cities, factories and mines. Some animals are still able to survive in the changed landscapes. Farms, for example, can provide new types of food for wildlife. But they are unlikely to have lots of wild animals unless they still have plenty of trees, hedgerows and other wild corners to provide shelter.

People do not even have to destroy habitats to make them unsuitable for animals. Sometimes a few changes simply make life too difficult. Dams on rivers, for instance, stop fish moving up and downstream. Too many cattle or sheep put out to pasture in natural grasslands can thin out the foliage too much for wildlife because of grazing and trampling.

The loss of some habitats is particularly worrying. Wetlands such as marshes, bogs and swamps are disappearing fast all over the world as people drain the water from them or fill them with earth. Afterward the soil is dry enough for farming or other uses, but many kinds of water creatures and birds will have lost their homes. Tropical forests are the only habitat for millions of animal species, but they, too, are shrinking year by year because the trees are being chopped down for wood and cleared away to make space for farms, ranches and plantations. Even if the plots are later abandoned, plants grow poorly in the sun-baked soil. Centuries may pass before forests once again cover the land.

Pollution is another serious threat to wildlife, especially in areas where lots of people live. Carelessly thrown away rubbish, sewage and chemicals contaminate the soil, rivers and the sea, and gases from factories and cars pollute the air. Too much pollution can ruin an animal's habitat and even kill it if it gets into its body. If farmers spray a strong chemical on their crops to kill pests, it can poison lots of other animals that live around farms because the chemical enters the food they eat.

Animals also die directly at the hands of people through hunting and fishing. Wild animals are killed for food, for sport and for their skin, fur, horns or shells. Too many hunters chasing one particular kind of animal may wipe it out entirely. Farmers also have guns and set traps to protect their crops and livestock from wild animals. Wolves, for

The terrible oil spills and fires started during the 1991 Gulf War destroyed countless animals. Many birds migrating across the area were also killed. Some were coated with soot from the thick smoke. Others died when they flew down to the oil lakes, mistaking the gleaming surface for water.

Oil pollution at sea is dangerous for wildlife because it forms a thick layer, or slick, on top of the water. Any bird that swims on to it gets its feathers so matted with oil that it cannot fly away. When it tries to clean its plumage with its bill it is likely to swallow so much oil that it dies.

instance, have long been persecuted wherever they occur because people fear that they attack farm animals. As a result, many species of wolf are now endangered.

Parrots and tortoises both make popular pets. But catching them and keeping them in captivity depletes their wild populations, especially if there are lots of pet shops overseas that want to buy them. Several species of parrots and tortoises, as well as other animals, have become endangered because of this. Wild apes are still captured for medical experiments although this trade is now illegal. One of the saddest things about the capture of wildlife is that many of the animals that are caught and taken away from their natural home die before they reach their destination.

Transporting animals around the world can itself be a threat to wildlife, especially if they are set free to roam wild in their new home. Releasing animals, on purpose or accidentally, in places where they did not live before is called introduction. People have taken cats, dogs and farm animals with them around the world and some of them now roam free in the wild. Rabbits have been released in new areas to provide food, fur and sport for hunters, and rats have spread around the world on their own by escaping from ships. An introduced animal can be dangerous because it may not have any natural enemies to keep its numbers down. It can easily upset the balance of nature by eating too much of another animal's food or being too good at hunting native wildlife.

Counting the cost

It is normal in nature for animals to rise and fall in number. Occasionally one kind may die out completely, becoming extinct. But changes like this usually happen very slowly over many generations. In today's world, however, the threats to wildlife are so great that thousands upon thousands of species are becoming scarce at the same time.

Some types of animals are especially vulnerable to threats. Large animals, such as rhinoceroses, need plenty of wild habitat to live in and their numbers are not very high in the first place. Because poachers can make a big profit by selling rhino horn they are ready to go far and wide to find the animals, and so all the rhinos in a large area can be killed off in a short time. Together, the five species of rhinoceros once ranged over most of Africa and tropical Asia, but today they have disappeared from all but a handful of places.

Other species are at risk because they live only in one place. Their original home might be a single lake, an isolated patch of forest or a far-flung island. If people start to hunt one of these animals or ruin its habitat, it has nowhere else to hide and may quickly die out. Even if the threat is stopped it may be too late. The animal's population may already be so low that an outbreak of disease, a powerful storm or any other natural disaster could easily finish it off.

Distant island animals are especially vulnerable for another reason. Because they are hard to reach, islands usually have far fewer species on them than the mainland. The animals that do live there may not have many natural enemies and are not adapted for defending themselves from attack. This makes them easy prey for human hunters and new animals such as rats and cats that people introduce to the islands. In fact, there are so many endangered animals on islands that they have a chapter at the end of the book all to themselves.

Keeping a record of which animals are endangered is one of the jobs of the IUCN, the International Union for Conservation of Nature and Natural Resources. By collecting together lots of information on an animal species thought to be endangered, the IUCN can work out roughly how much its population has fallen in recent years, what sorts of threats it faces, and whether anything is being done to protect it. Then it can say how badly the animal is threatened and what more could be done to try to save it. The IUCN's Red Data Books are a good way of finding out which of the world's animals are in danger.

The Philippine eagle is one of the world's most endangered birds. There are probably fewer than 200 of these magnificent birds of prey left in the wild. A powerful predator big enough to catch monkeys, the eagle needs large areas of rainforest in which to hunt. But much of its home in the Philippines has already been destroyed and the rest is under threat from logging.

ENDANGERED SPECIES

Here are some of the birds and mammals in this book that are currently in the most grave danger of dying out for ever:

Eskimo curlew

Kauai o-o

Ivory-billed woodpecker

Indigo macaw

Mountain gorilla

Madagascar fish eagle

Hermit ibis

Mediterranean monk seal

Baiji dolphin

Sumatran rhinoceros

White-eyed river martin

Kakapo

EXTINCT ANIMALS

Great auk

Dodo

Steller's sea cow

Quagga

Some animals have already been driven to extinction. Over the last 400 years, about one kind of mammal or bird has disappeared from the earth every year, including such fascinating creatures as the great auk and the dodo (both flightless birds), Steller's sea cow (a giant water mammal) and the quagga (a half-striped zebra). Many more animals all over the world are now endangered—their numbers have fallen so low that they, too, are likely to die out and follow these animals into extinction.

Saving species

Just as people are responsible for putting the future of so many animals at risk, so we have the power to make their future safer. It is very difficult to stop the things that threaten wildlife but lots of people now want to give endangered species a chance to survive. Actions to help wild animals are called wildlife conservation.

One of the simplest steps of wildlife conservation is to make laws that reduce or stop the killing and hunting of threatened animals. Most nations have such laws. When strictly enforced, they give threatened or endangered animals a chance to recover. Sometimes, international controls are needed, like the 1986 agreement to stop all whaling across the world.

CITES stands for the Convention on International Trade in Endangered Species of Wild Fauna and Flora. No fewer than 112 countries belong to CITES and they meet regularly to decide controls for all kinds of threatened wildlife. Many species are listed in CITES' highest category, which means that no country should allow animal traders to take them into or out of its ports. This includes live or stuffed specimens and any products from the animals such as meat, shells, skins or horns.

But bans and controls do not always work. Many protected animals are still shot illegally by poachers, and it is sometimes quite easy to smuggle them abroad. Some people are prepared to break wildlife laws, especially if others will pay them lots of money for the animals or for animal products. One answer to this is to allow people to breed a threatened animal in captivity and sell the captive or farmed animals rather than take ones from the wild population. This has already helped some species of crocodiles and alligators, which are farmed in large numbers for their meat and hide.

Other ways of protecting individual species can cost a lot of time and money, and it is mainly in the richer countries that conservation groups have the means to do them. In New Zealand, where introduced animals threaten lots of native wildlife,

The efforts of campaigning groups such as Greenpeace have helped give the world's great whales a chance to recover after years of intensive whaling. In 1986 the International Whaling Commission agreed to stop all commercial hunting of whales after a lot of pressure from people and organizations all over the world. Several species, including the mighty blue whale, had been hunted so ruthlessly that they were fast heading toward extinction.

Even though there has been no commercial whaling since 1986 it will take many more years for the populations of great whales to build up. And, already, some countries want to start hunting the whales again.

conservationists have rounded up several highly endangered species and flown them to offshore islands that are free of rats and other threats.

If a species is in grave danger in the wild and is unlikely to survive, the only way to save it from extinction may be to capture some animals and keep them safe in captivity, often in zoos. Conservationists then need to encourage them to mate and raise young, which is not always easy because the animals may not breed in the unnatural conditions of captivity.

If captive-breeding is successful there may be enough animals after several generations to try setting a few free again in the wild. This is called reintroduction and has already brought some animals, like the Arabian oryx, back from virtual extinction. Great care has to be taken to make sure the animals still know how to fend for themselves in the wild and do not rely on people for food. For reintroductions to work, the original reason for the animal's decline must no longer be a threat.

Reintroducing animals bred in captivity into the wild is one way to help endangered species. The Arabian oryx was killed off in the wild by hunters wanting its magnificent horns. But now captive-born herds have been successfully released in Oman where they are protected from hunting and disturbance. Hopefully, these animals will survive and breed in the wild.

CONSERVATION AND CONTROVERSY

Most people feel it's important to save wildlife, but sometimes conservation appears to interfere with other important things. If, for example, people make a living by cutting down trees, they may fear that the protection of an endangered species puts their jobs in jeopardy. Businesses making large profits from an industry may not want to change their practices in order to preserve species, either. Governments may become involved in resolving these issues. Because of such difficulties, saving wildlife is often not easy. The case of the northern spotted owl shows what can happen when conservation clashes with big business.

There may be only 3,000 pairs of the northern spotted owl left in the forests along the Pacific coast of North America. Logging is destroying the owl's habitat, and if it continues, the owl will soon be extinct. The timber companies believe that cutting trees brings needed money to the Pacific Northwest. Loggers are concerned that they will lose their jobs if forests are preserved for the owl. The United States government has authorized limited logging, but neither loggers nor conservationists are satisfied with this decision, and controversy continues.

Saving habitats

Most conservationists agree that the single most important thing that can be done to save the world's wildlife is to preserve natural habitats. Wild animals cannot survive without them anyway, and by saving a habitat a number of animal and plant species can be helped at the same time.

One of the best ways to do this is to turn a natural landscape into a reserve—a place set aside for nature. Inside a reserve, habitat destruction should either be kept to a minimum or not allowed at all. A reserve can also be a refuge from hunters, and one of the jobs of the people who run a reserve is to guard it from harmful intruders.

Today there are many thousands of reserves around the world protecting forests, grasslands, deserts, mountains, wetlands, seashores and coral reefs. They range in size from tiny sanctuaries of a few hectares, perhaps protecting a single marsh or a patch of woodland, to giant national parks covering thousands of square kilometres where a variety of different habitats are preserved.

Some reserves have been set up by individual people—in fact, some of the oldest ones were parts of estates set aside by landowners as places where they could hunt deer and game for sport. Others have been set up by charities devoted to conservation, such as the international World Wide Fund for Nature. Many of the biggest are run by governments, which usually have a department responsible for wildlife and national parks.

Some reserves are strictly the home of wildlife and few people are allowed to go inside. Others, especially the big national parks, may have communities living and working in them and they can attract lots of visitors. If so, people's impact on the habitat and any disturbance of wildlife needs to be carefully controlled.

Unfortunately, many reserves and national parks are not protected well enough. Guards and rangers cannot always stop intruders coming into reserves to poach animals. Also, governments sometimes allow companies to cut trees for timber or to dig mines inside national parks as a way of raising money. Natural landscapes are always popular with tourists, and if a reserve is home for spectacular animals, such as gorillas, bears, or flocks of beautiful parrots, visitors will come and see them and pay an admission fee which may profit the reserve. Great care has to be taken, however, that the number of visitors does not harm the reserve or its inhabitants.

But even good reserves are not enough to save the great variety of wildlife on our planet well into the future. Less than 4 percent of all the world's land is protected. If the remaining 96 percent became suitable only for humans to live in we would lose countless numbers of species. Reserves are very

Yellowstone, the world's oldest national park (left) is also one of the largest. It covers 8,900 square kilometres of mountains, forests, meadows, lakes and canyons in the western United States. Though many people visit the park, great efforts are made to ensure that they do as little damage as possible to the park's wildlife habitats. As a result, the park is a huge, safe home for animals such as bald eagles, grizzly bears, bighorn sheep and American bison.

Conserving habitats helps wildlife everywhere, even in crowded cities. In many urban areas people have removed rubbish and dug ponds to help turn waste ground into attractive refuges for a variety of animals from butterflies to foxes (below). A thoughtfully planted garden can also attract wildlife and even the tiniest garden pond can make a home for dragonflies and frogs.

important for saving the best bits of wilderness that are left, but we must also find ways of letting wildlife continue to live alongside us.

There are various things that can be tried. Timber companies, for example, can cut down and remove trees in ways that do not destroy whole forests. Trees can be replanted where they used to grow and better methods can be found of getting rid of our waste so that it does not pollute rivers.

More and more people realize the importance of doing something for wildlife now before it is too late. In 1992, governments from all over the world met in Rio de Janeiro, Brazil, to discuss the future of our planet. One of the things they agreed on was the need for wealthy countries to help others protect their plants and animals.

North America and the Caribbean

Efforts to save wildlife from extinction started more than a century ago in North America.

People were worried about the future of North America's wildlife as long ago as 1872, when the famous Yellowstone National Park was founded. At that time birds were hunted so ruthlessly for their meat that some, such as the passenger pigeon, became extinct. Other animals, such as buffalo, were shot in huge numbers.

Since then, the continent's wildlife has faced even greater dangers because its natural habitats are being destroyed. Today, most of the rolling prairie is used for farmland. Two-thirds of the tropical forests of Central America have been cut down to make way for plantations and farms. Pine forests are being stripped away by logging companies.

Pollution has made many traditional habitats difficult places to live. The Great Lakes of Canada and the United States have been so badly polluted by waste from the cities around their shores that many animals have died. Sewage and oil have killed large stretches of coral in the Caribbean Sea.

But help is at hand. There are now controls on hunting and pollution. Hundreds of nature reserves like Yellowstone have been established. And, in Central America, people are replanting tropical forests on unused farm plots.

Bald eagles became rare because they fed on fish contaminated with the chemical DDT. This made their eggshells so thin that few hatched safely. Now that DDT is banned, the eagle population is recovering.

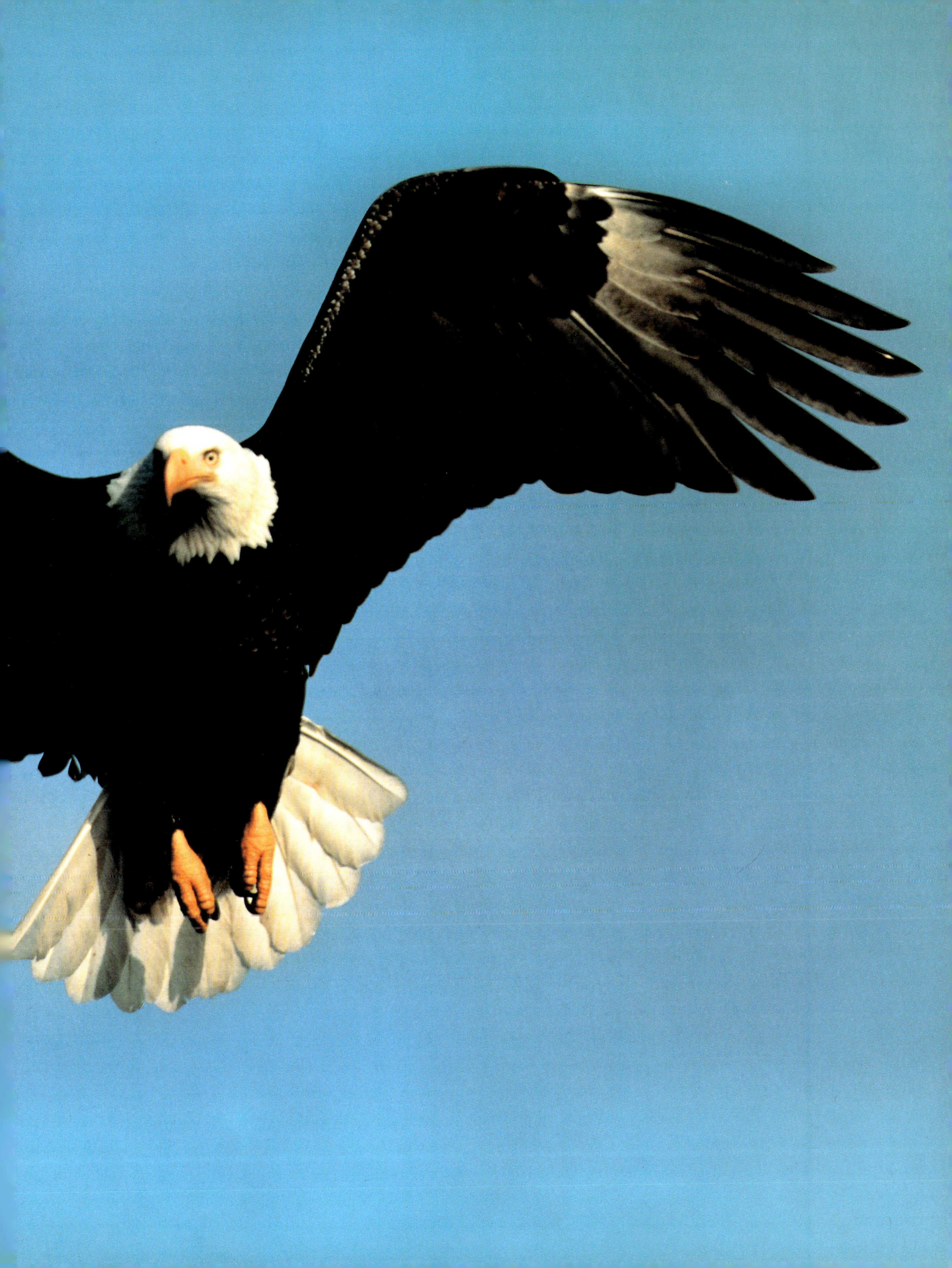

Threatened animals of North America and the Caribbean

The threatened wildlife of North America and the Caribbean shows us just how hard it is for some animals to share the world with people. The cougar, for example, has become extremely rare in many regions because its hunting grounds have been turned into fields or settlements. And although the cougar seldom attacks farm animals—its usual prey is deer and smaller wild animals—farmers often kill it to protect their herds. The West Indian manatee is in danger all round the Caribbean. It lives in lagoons, estuaries and on coasts, often where people are busily using the water. Lots of manatees die every year when they collide with motor boats, are caught in fishing nets and are harmed by pollution.

The volcano rabbit lives only on the grassy slopes of a few high volcanoes near Mexico City. But farmers' fields are advancing uphill and taking over its home, and people hunt the rabbits for food. Hunting has also made the Central American river turtle rare. People say its meat tastes like chicken breast and it has become so popular in parts of Mexico that an

① Blue-headed quail dove

⑥ Volcano rabbit

⑦ American bison

North America

② Central American river turtle

airstrip has been built near one river so that tonnes of wild turtle meat can be flown out every year.

One of the most serious problems in tropical countries is the rapid disappearance of forests. Lots of animals that live in them cannot survive anywhere else. The blue-headed quail dove forages on the floor of tall, shady forests where there is not too much undergrowth. But on Cuba, where it lives, old, untouched forest like this is rare.

Finding money for conservation is not easy in the poorer countries around the Caribbean. But in the north there have been some famous success stories. The American bison, which was almost wiped out by hunting, has been carefully protected this century in places like the Yellowstone and Wood Buffalo national parks. Now there are about 100,000 of them. The last wild Californian condors were actually captured in 1987 to save them from the risk of being shot, poisoned or accidentally killed. Since then the surviving birds have bred so well in zoos that two have been set free. Conservationists hope to release more condors back into the wild soon.

③ West Indian manatee

⑤ Cougar

④ Californian condor

Spotted salamander

Spotted salamanders spend most of their time well out of sight, burrowing through damp soil, but every spring they gather in writhing crowds around pools to mate and lay eggs in the water. Sadly, this spectacle no longer occurs in many areas because air pollution is creating acid rain. Dangerous chemicals then spill into the breeding pools and kill both eggs and young salamanders.

FOUND IN:
Eastern North America

MAIN THREAT:
Pollution

SCIENTIFIC NAME:
Ambystoma maculatum

SIZE:
15–25 cm long

Cuban solenodon

The Cuban solenodon emerges at night to snatch insects from the forest floor. It is now rare—it has been attacked by introduced predators such as cats and has suffered from the clearance of trees. Three of the areas in which it lives are now nature reserves.

FOUND IN:
Cuba

MAIN THREATS:
Introduced animals and habitat destruction

SCIENTIFIC NAME:
Solenodon cubanus

SIZE:
Body 28–33 cm long, tail 17–25 cm

FOUND IN:
Cuba

MAIN THREAT:
Habitat destruction

SCIENTIFIC NAME:
Campephilus principalis

SIZE:
45–50 cm long

FOREST AND WOODLAND ANIMALS

Ingraham's hutia

FOUND IN:
Bahamas

SCIENTIFIC NAME:
Geocapromys ingrahami

SIZE:
37–39 cm long

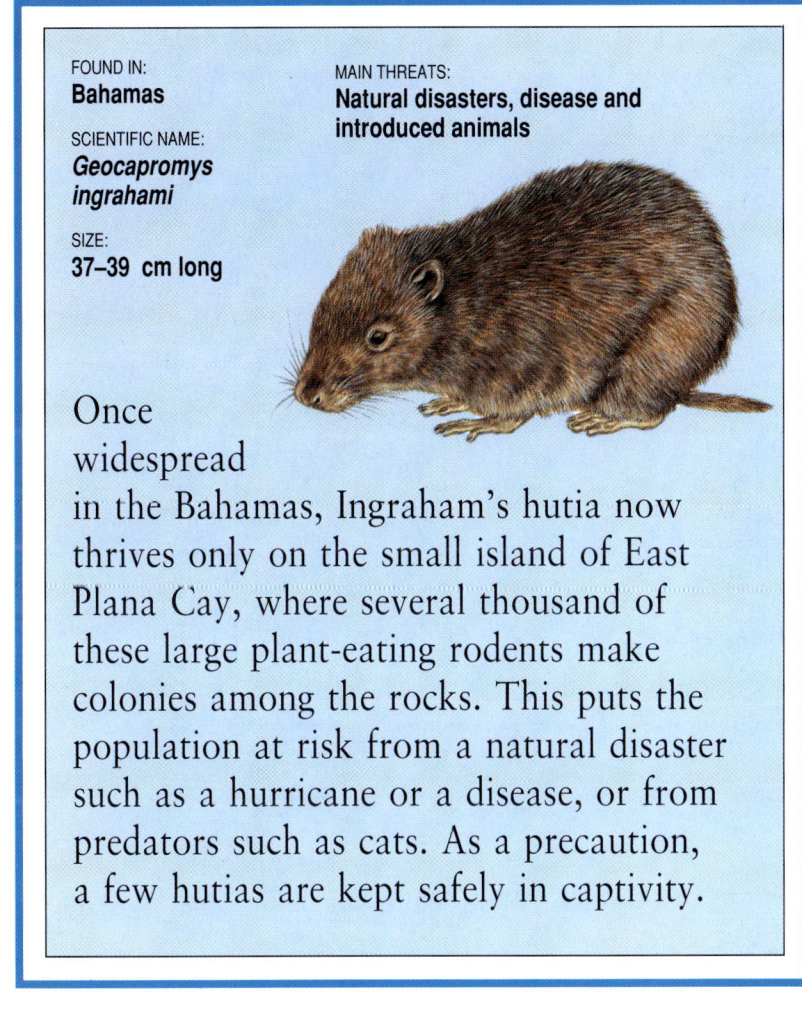

MAIN THREATS:
Natural disasters, disease and introduced animals

Once widespread in the Bahamas, Ingraham's hutia now thrives only on the small island of East Plana Cay, where several thousand of these large plant-eating rodents make colonies among the rocks. This puts the population at risk from a natural disaster such as a hurricane or a disease, or from predators such as cats. As a precaution, a few hutias are kept safely in captivity.

Ivory-billed woodpecker

This striking woodpecker can only survive in large stretches of old, undisturbed woodland. Many years of forest felling have therefore driven it close to extinction. Today, only a few remain in a remote pine forest reserve in eastern Cuba. There may also be some in the dense swamp forests of Louisiana or Florida, although the last definite sighting in the United States was in 1946.

Resplendent quetzal

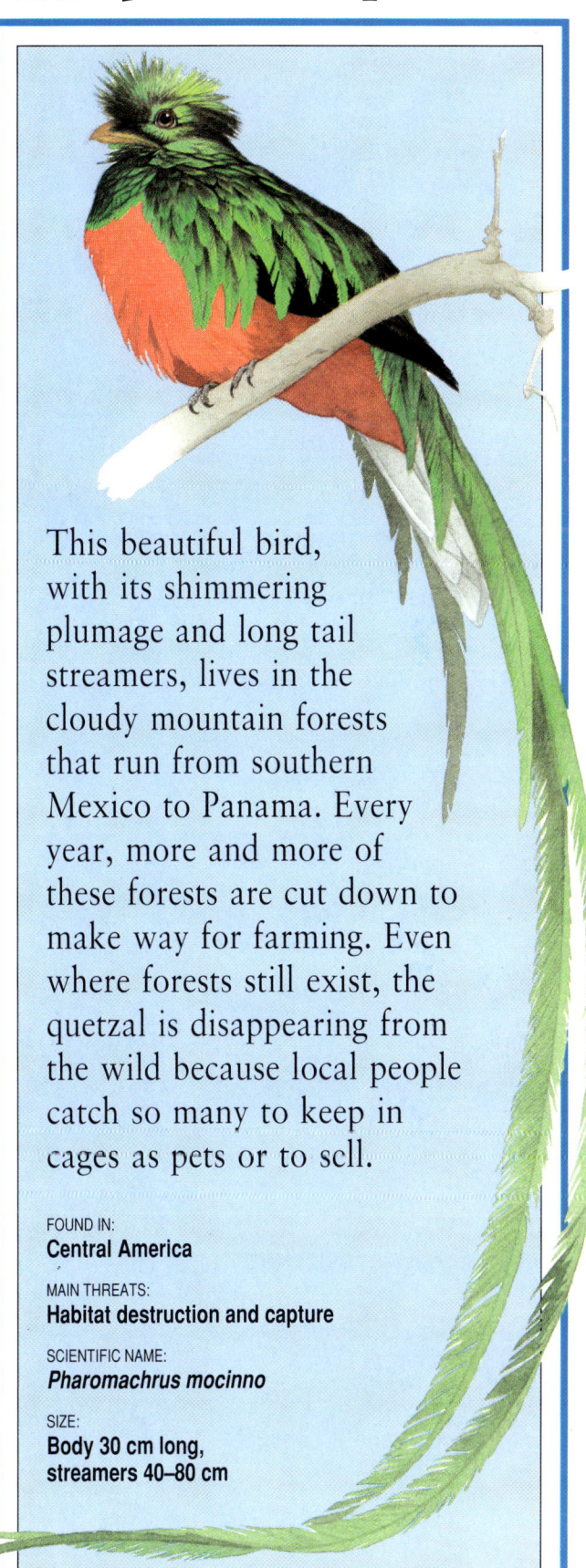

This beautiful bird, with its shimmering plumage and long tail streamers, lives in the cloudy mountain forests that run from southern Mexico to Panama. Every year, more and more of these forests are cut down to make way for farming. Even where forests still exist, the quetzal is disappearing from the wild because local people catch so many to keep in cages as pets or to sell.

FOUND IN:
Central America

MAIN THREATS:
Habitat destruction and capture

SCIENTIFIC NAME:
Pharomachrus mocinno

SIZE:
Body 30 cm long, streamers 40–80 cm

Focus on: *Kemp's ridley turtle*

All the world's sea turtles are threatened by hunting, but Kemp's ridley has come closest to extinction. In the past, huge numbers of female turtles used to come ashore together to lay their eggs on the long sandy beach at Rancho Nuevo in Mexico. In 1947 as many as 40,000 turtles crowded on the sand during one mass nesting. But this amazing sight was not to last for long. More and more local people started to hunt the turtles and dig up their eggs from the beach, either to feed their families or to sell the meat and eggs in markets. Lots of these people were poor and hungry, but they took so many that the turtles began to disappear fast.

Far fewer turtles came to lay their eggs on the Rancho Nuevo beach at any one time. By 1989 the total number of turtles coming ashore had plunged below 400. Today, hunting is banned and efforts are being made to protect Kemp's ridley but its future is still uncertain.

Every turtle counts
Though lots of people want to save sea turtles, Kemp's ridley is still in great danger. Today the main threats to the turtles are accidental. Lots of them are injured or killed when they become caught in nets used to catch shrimps and fish.

Getting a headstart
To give Kemp's ridley as much chance as possible to recover, thousands of baby turtles are reared in special hatcheries in Texas and Mexico before being released into the sea. This should help the population because, in the wild, lots of eggs and young hatchlings are eaten by predators.

The hazards of nesting
Every year, between April and July, Kemp's ridley turtles lay their eggs on a single stretch of beach in Mexico. In the past people used to lie in wait for them, ready to steal the eggs and kill the turtles as they slowly hauled themselves back toward the sea. Now there are special armed patrols on the beach to protect the nesting turtles from poachers.

Black-footed ferret

FOUND IN:
Central United States

SCIENTIFIC NAME:
Mustela nigripes

SIZE:
50–53 cm long

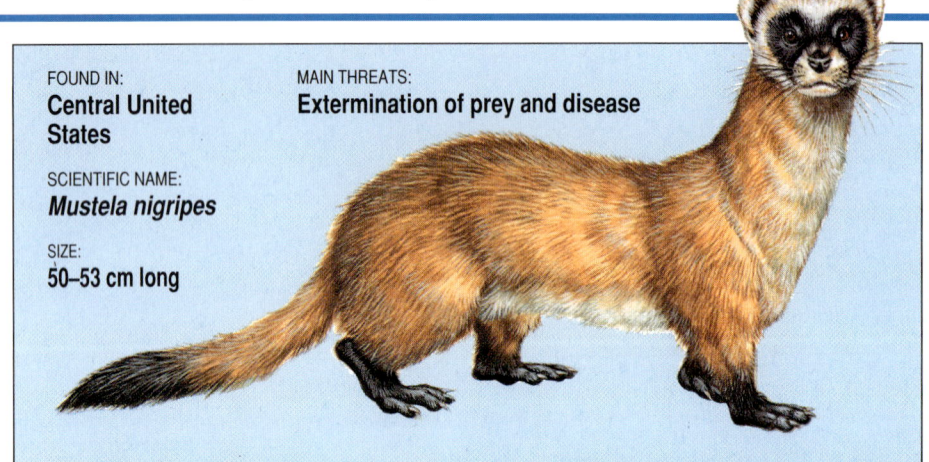

MAIN THREATS:
Extermination of prey and disease

When farmers began killing prairie dogs to protect cattle pastures, the black-footed ferret was doomed. Starved by the disappearance of its prey, prone to disease, and accidentally poisoned, it nearly died out altogether. In 1986, the last few wild ferrets were rounded up, but since then they have bred so well in captivity that there are now about 300. Some are being returned to the wild.

FOUND IN:
Western Mexico

SCIENTIFIC NAME:
Brachypelma smithii

MAIN THREAT:
Capture

SIZE:
Up to 17 cm legspan

Pronghorn

There may once have been more than 40 million pronghorns grazing the American prairies. Hunting brought this number down to fewer than 20,000 by the 1920s. Strict protection came just in time, and today the population has increased to almost half a million in the United States. But in Mexico pronghorns are still in danger from hunters and the loss of their habitat to cattle and horses.

FOUND IN:
Western North America

SCIENTIFIC NAME:
Antilocapra americana

MAIN THREATS:
Hunting and habitat destruction

SIZE:
1–1.5 m long

GRASSLAND AND DESERT ANIMALS

Red-kneed tarantula

This impressive spider lives in burrows in the dry lands of Mexico. Colourful, docile and harmless to people, it is becoming a popular, exotic pet. Local people are starting to collect so many for export to the United States and Europe that the spiders could soon become very scarce in the wild. Conservationists say there should be much stronger controls on this trade.

Eskimo curlew

FOUND IN:
Northern Canada and Alaska

MAIN THREAT:
Hunting

SCIENTIFIC NAME:
Numenius borealis

SIZE:
29–34 cm long

Huge flocks of eskimo curlews used to migrate every year from the northern tundra to their wintering grounds in South America. Today, the bird is almost extinct because so many have been shot by hunters. Small numbers are still spotted every few years and shooting is banned, but these measures are probably too late to save this species.

Rhinoceros iguana

This lizard, which gets its name from the pointed scales on its snout, lives only on Hispaniola and its small neighbour Mona Island. Its future is threatened by the spread of villages and farms and by the various animals that have been taken to the islands. Donkeys and goats browse and trample on the scrubby vegetation in which it hides, and pigs, dogs, cats and mongooses eat its eggs and attack its young.

FOUND IN: **West Indies**

MAIN THREATS: **Habitat destruction and introduced animals**

SCIENTIFIC NAME: *Cyclura cornuta*

SIZE: **Up to 1.2 m long**

NORTH AMERICA

Grey whale

For more than 300 years, grey whales were at the mercy of whaling ships. They became extinct as early as the seventeenth century in the North Atlantic and even now number fewer than 200 in the entire western Pacific. As a result of careful protection, the population in the eastern Pacific has increased to 21,000. These whales make a round-trip migration of 20,000 km every year between the cold waters off the coast of Alaska, where they spend the summer, and the subtropical shores of Mexico, their winter home.

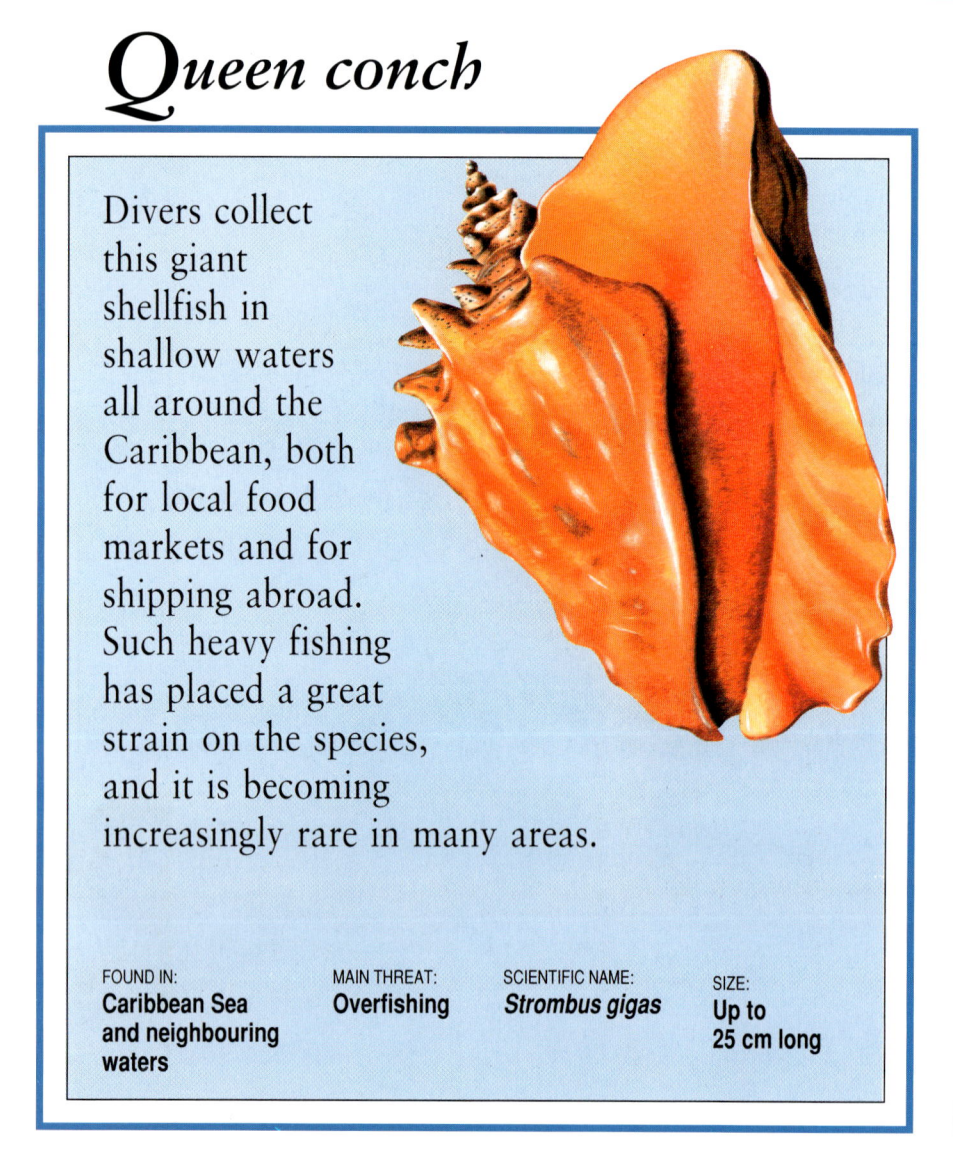

Queen conch

Divers collect this giant shellfish in shallow waters all around the Caribbean, both for local food markets and for shipping abroad. Such heavy fishing has placed a great strain on the species, and it is becoming increasingly rare in many areas.

FOUND IN:	MAIN THREAT:	SCIENTIFIC NAME:	SIZE:
Caribbean Sea and neighbouring waters	Overfishing	*Strombus gigas*	Up to 25 cm long

Whooping crane

In 1941, there were just 15 whooping cranes left in the wild, due to hunting and the drainage of their marshland habitats. Since then, strict hunting bans, protection of nesting and wintering sites, captive-breeding and even the use of other wild cranes as foster parents for chicks, have gradually built up the number again to 140 in the wild. But the whooping crane is still in serious danger of extinction.

FRESHWATER AND SEA ANIMALS

FOUND IN:
Eastern Pacific Ocean

SCIENTIFIC NAME:
Eschrichtius robustus

MAIN THREAT:
Hunting

SIZE:
10–15 m long

American alligator

FOUND IN:
Northern Canada and southern United States

MAIN THREATS:
Habitat destruction and hunting

SCIENTIFIC NAME:
Grus americana

SIZE:
1.2–1.4 m long

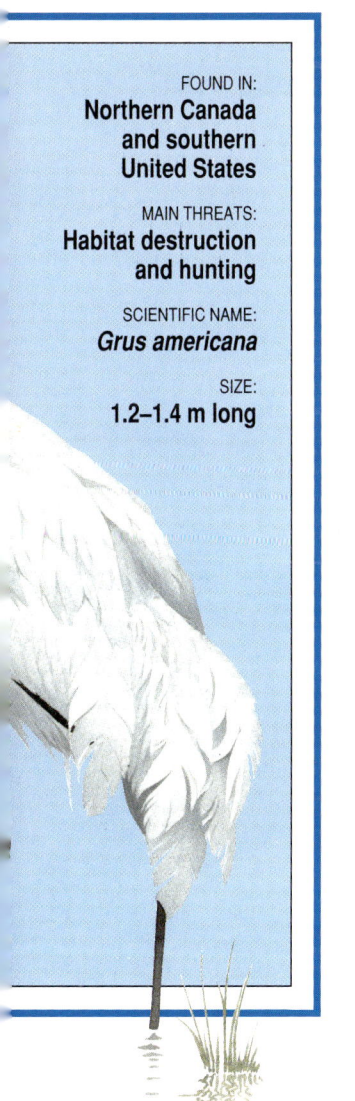

Efforts to conserve the American alligator have been very successful. Earlier this century alligators were close to extinction because hunters killed so many for their skins. Trading companies used to sell up to 60,000 skins a year to be made into shoes, belts and bags. With hunting banned, there are now at least 800,000 alligators in the wild.

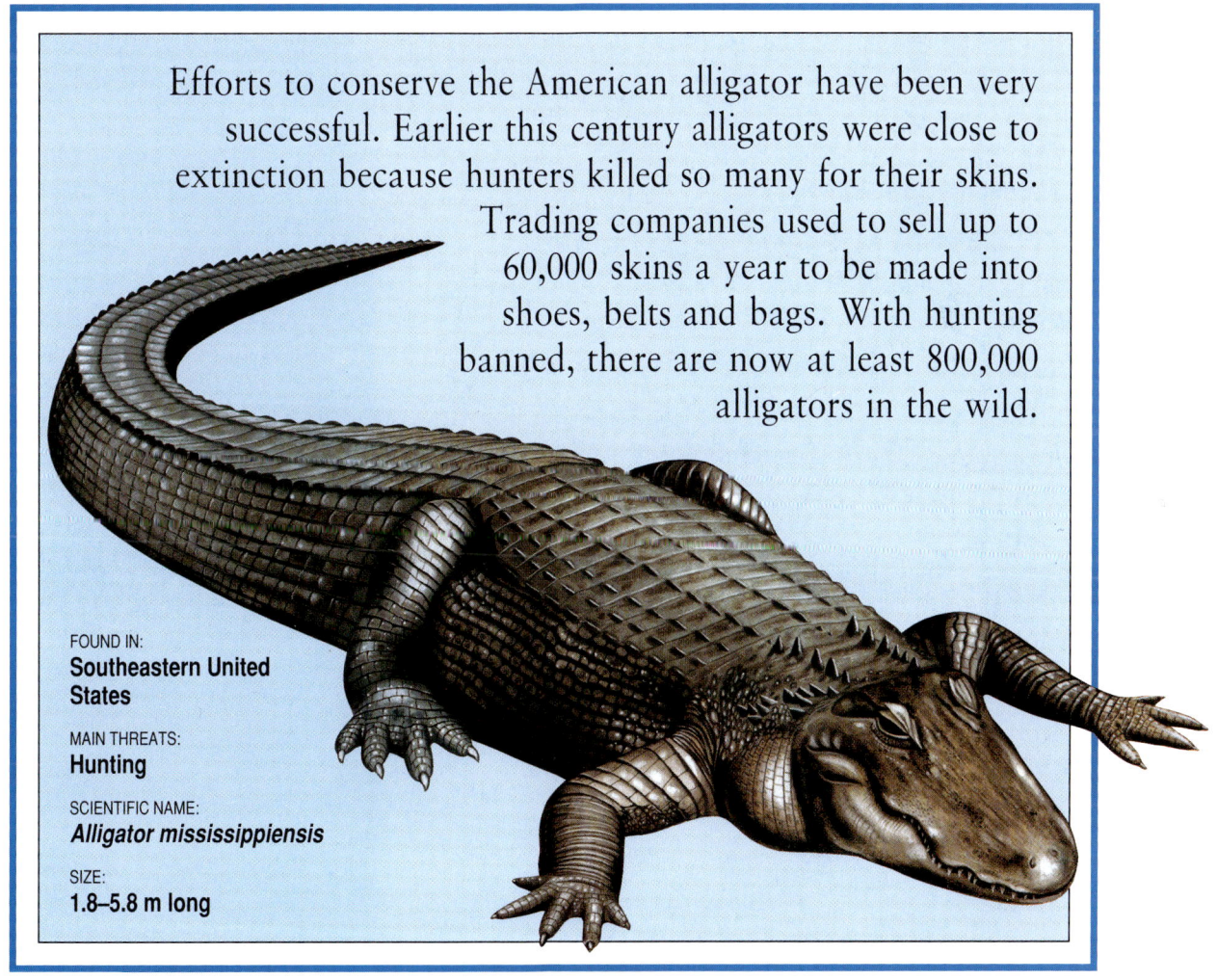

FOUND IN:
Southeastern United States

MAIN THREATS:
Hunting

SCIENTIFIC NAME:
Alligator mississippiensis

SIZE:
1.8–5.8 m long

South America

The wild landscapes of South America are changing fast. Even the world's greatest rainforest is in danger.

Three-quarters of South America is still covered by woodland, forest, savanna or desert, and is teeming with fascinating wildlife. Today, however, this wilderness is threatened more and more.

Because the population is growing and land is scarce, people are forced into the wild to find new farming plots. Piece by piece the wilderness is disappearing. Those who settle there go into the surrounding habitats to hunt animals. They hunt for food, or for skins to sell, but also to capture monkeys or parrots to sell as pets.

All these activities are dangerous for wildlife. Many of the animals that live in the Andes Mountains are threatened by hunting and the spread of pasture. In the lowland savannas, grazing by cattle has made the grass too short to hide animals like the pampas deer.

But the greatest problems are in the rainforests. In the great Amazon forest ranchers, settlers, logging companies and huge industrial projects are destroying one of the richest wildlife habitats on Earth. In the 1980s, about 22,000 square kilometres of forest were burned away every year. This is about the same area as Brazil's Jau National Park, one of several reserves in the Amazon. In the future these protected areas will become even more important to protect South America's natural landscapes and animal and bird life.

The golden lion tamarin has lost almost all of its rainforest habitat and more than half of the animals alive today are in zoos. Some of these are now being released into protected areas of the forest.

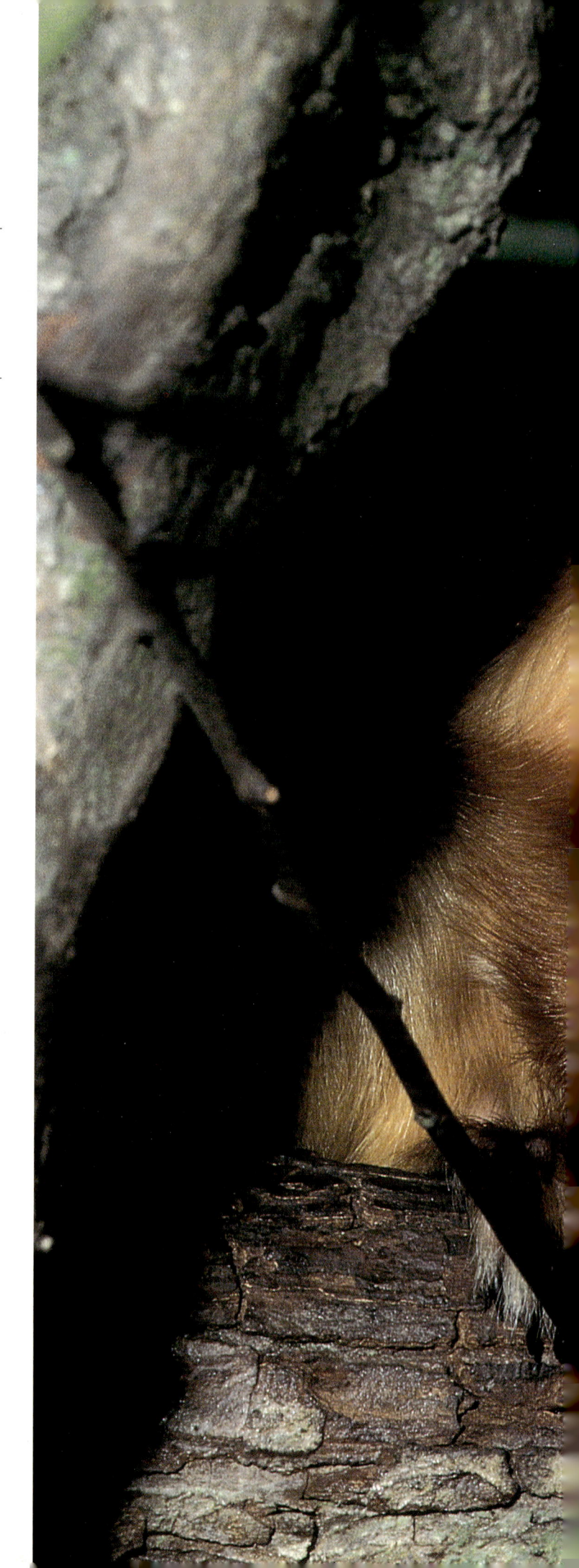

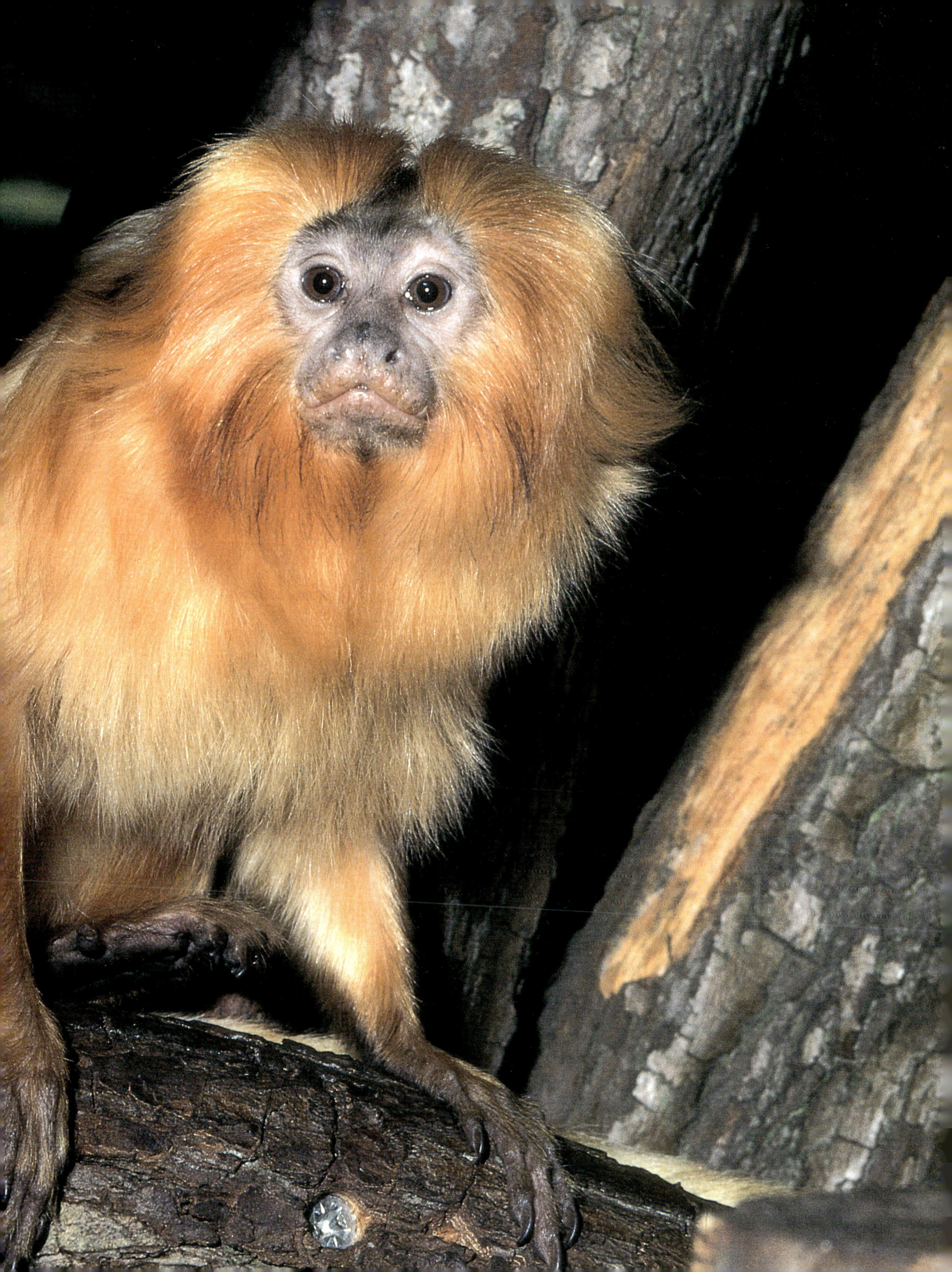

South America's threatened animals

Most endangered animals in South America are at risk for two reasons. Large parts of their habitat are being destroyed and, where their habitat does remain, people hunt the animals in large numbers. The jaguar, which needs a big area of rainforest in which to find enough prey, no longer has enough space in many areas because so much of the forest has been cut down. If it appears near settlements, hunters may kill it to protect cattle and for its beautiful fur.

The pig-like Chaco peccary lives in drier, thorny forests, but these too are being cleared fast to make way for crops and cattle pasture. Hunters, meanwhile, find peccaries easy to shoot for their meat because they bunch together when danger threatens. Drained marshes and straightened, obstructed and polluted rivers have become unsuitable for the broad-nosed caiman. This small crocodile has also been hunted heavily for its hide, which is usually smuggled abroad.

Animals with low populations or small ranges are always at risk. The indigo macaw lives in a dry area of northeastern Brazil, where its main food is the nut of one particular palm. The spread of cattle farming has made the palms hard to find. To make things worse, people sometimes catch these lovely parrots and send them to collectors overseas. Now

① White uakari

⑦ Jaguar

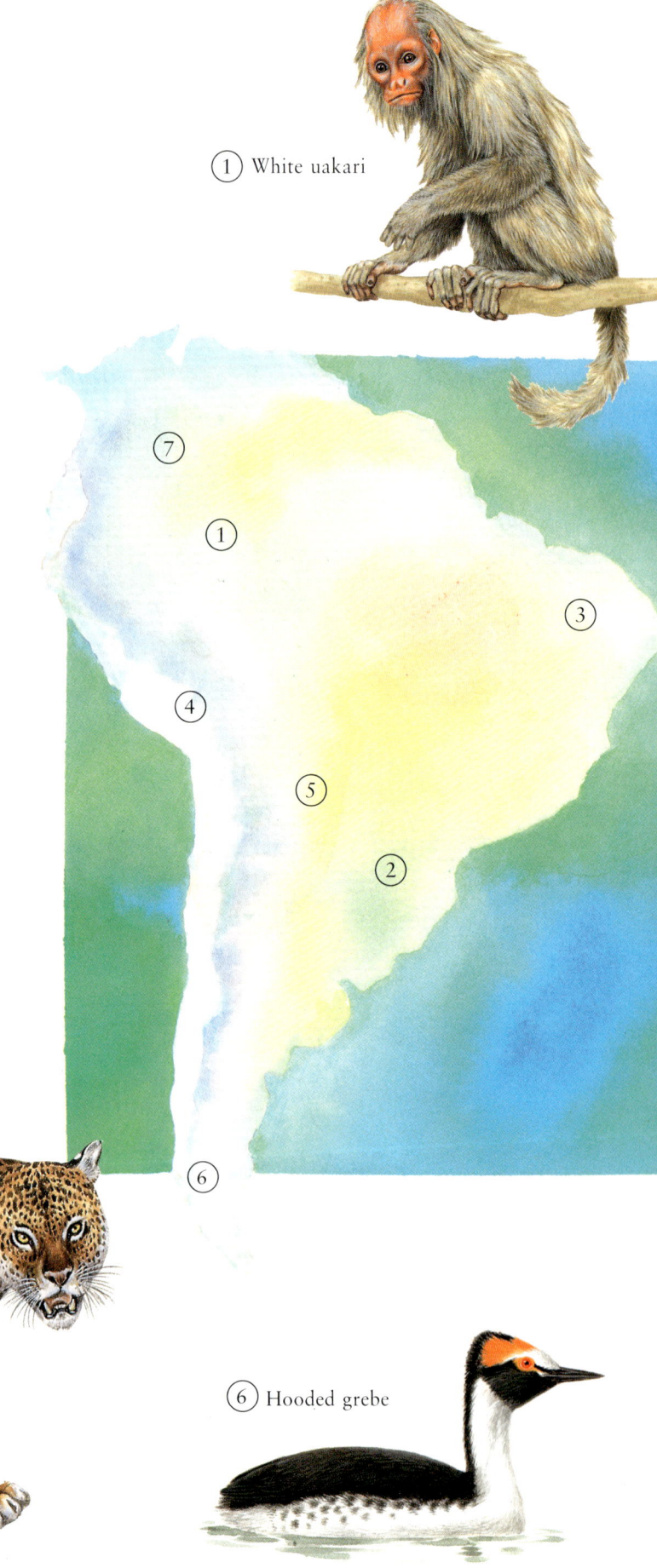

⑥ Hooded grebe

South America

② Broad-nosed caiman

only about 60 of them remain in the wild. The white uakari, an unusual monkey, is confined to a tiny area of rainforest bounded on all sides by wide rivers. Since its colour makes it a noticeable target, it could easily be killed off by hunters. The hooded grebe could be vulnerable to changes in its habitat if more people settle in Patagonia. There are probably no more than 5,000 of these birds scattered across large lakes in the region.

The jaguar and the indigo macaw are protected by nature reserves in parts of their range, but it is hard to make these places completely safe. The vicuna, a relative of the camel, has had better luck. By 1965, out of an original population of several million, only 6,000 vicunas remained in the high, bleak deserts of the Andes Mountains. But since then, with careful protection against poachers in special reserves, their numbers have risen to about 90,000.

③ Indigo macaw

④ Vicuna

⑤ Chaco peccary

31

SOUTH AMERICA

Woolly spider monkey

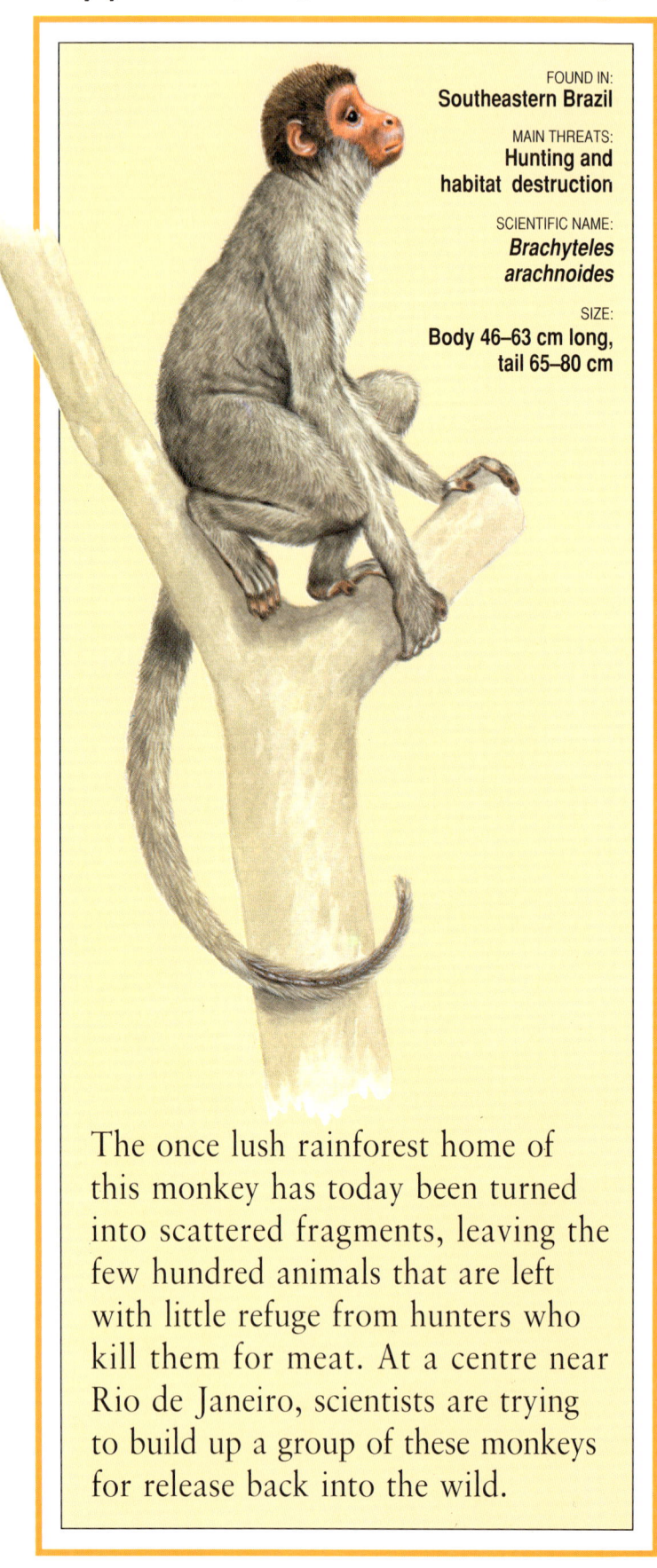

FOUND IN:
Southeastern Brazil

MAIN THREATS:
Hunting and habitat destruction

SCIENTIFIC NAME:
Brachyteles arachnoides

SIZE:
Body 46–63 cm long, tail 65–80 cm

The once lush rainforest home of this monkey has today been turned into scattered fragments, leaving the few hundred animals that are left with little refuge from hunters who kill them for meat. At a centre near Rio de Janeiro, scientists are trying to build up a group of these monkeys for release back into the wild.

Toucan barbet

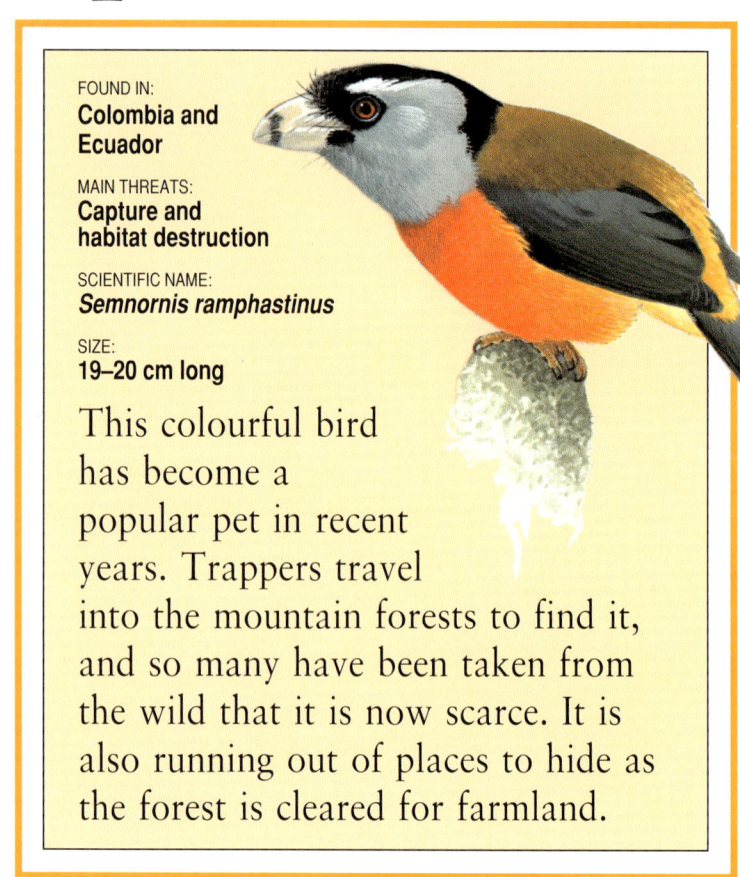

FOUND IN:
Colombia and Ecuador

MAIN THREATS:
Capture and habitat destruction

SCIENTIFIC NAME:
Semnornis ramphastinus

SIZE:
19–20 cm long

This colourful bird has become a popular pet in recent years. Trappers travel into the mountain forests to find it, and so many have been taken from the wild that it is now scarce. It is also running out of places to hide as the forest is cleared for farmland.

Marvellous spatuletail

Only the male spatuletail has these elaborate outer tail feathers. He uses them to try and impress a female by bending them forward and flying to and fro in front of her. Not a great deal is known about this remarkable bird. It seems to live only in the mountain forests of a small area of northern Peru—perhaps just a single valley. This means that the whole population is highly vulnerable to any changes in its habitat.

RAINFOREST ANIMALS

Emperor tamarin

Small troops of emperor tamarins dart through the trees looking for insects, fruit, tender leaves and even flowers to eat. These monkeys are rare in the western Amazon, and their numbers are likely to fall further still as stretches of forest disappear to make way for ranches. Their best chance of survival is in protected areas such as Peru's Manu National Park.

FOUND IN:
Western Brazil, Peru, Bolivia

SCIENTIFIC NAME:
Saguinus imperator

MAIN THREAT:
Habitat destruction

SIZE:
Body 23–26 cm long, tail 35–42 cm

Giant armadillo

The giant armadillo weighs up to 60 kg and is a powerful digger. It can easily burrow into ants' nests and break open termite mounds to feed on the swarming insects. But, because of its large size and tasty flesh, it is severely hunted in all areas where people also live. As more of its habitat disappears its decline is sure to continue.

FOUND IN:
Northern Peru

MAIN THREAT:
Habitat destruction

SCIENTIFIC NAME:
Loddigesia mirabilis

SIZE:
Body 10–12 cm long, tail up to 17 cm

FOUND IN:
Venezuela to northern Argentina

SCIENTIFIC NAME:
Priodontes maximus

MAIN THREATS:
Hunting and habitat destruction

SIZE:
Body 75 cm–1 m long, tail 40–50 cm

Focus on: Hyacinth macaw

It is easy to see why the hyacinth macaw is highly prized as a cage bird. It not only has gorgeous plumage but, at up to one metre long, it is also the longest of all the parrots. Pet traders can sell it for well over $10,000 in Europe or North America. But in the end, the beauty of this tropical bird has been its downfall.

Flocks of hyacinth macaws used to live all over the drier regions of Brazil, Bolivia and Paraguay. They started to decline because they were hunted for their meat and feathers and because farmers cut down many of their nesting and feeding trees. Since the 1960s, the greed of the pet trade has made things much worse. So many wild macaws have been trapped and sent abroad that there are now only about 3,000 left in all South America. They have completely disappeared from some areas. No more birds caught in the wild are supposed to be sold (only ones that have been bred in captivity), but, with big money at stake, smugglers are always ready to break the law.

Six macaws head overseas
Each year, several hundred hyacinth macaws are taken illegally out of South America. Although most countries have laws to control the trade, people still smuggle wild-caught parrots across seas and borders. The birds are often sent in bad, cramped conditions with little food or water.

Nest robbing
The hyacinth macaw is one of several South American parrots that are seriously endangered because of capture for the cage bird trade. Trappers catch adult macaws and also steal chicks from nests.

Spreading the message
Projects such as this painting on a school wall in Africa are important ways to help get local people interested in conservation. Colourful signs have been put up in parts of Brazil urging people not to harm the country's beautiful hyacinth macaw.

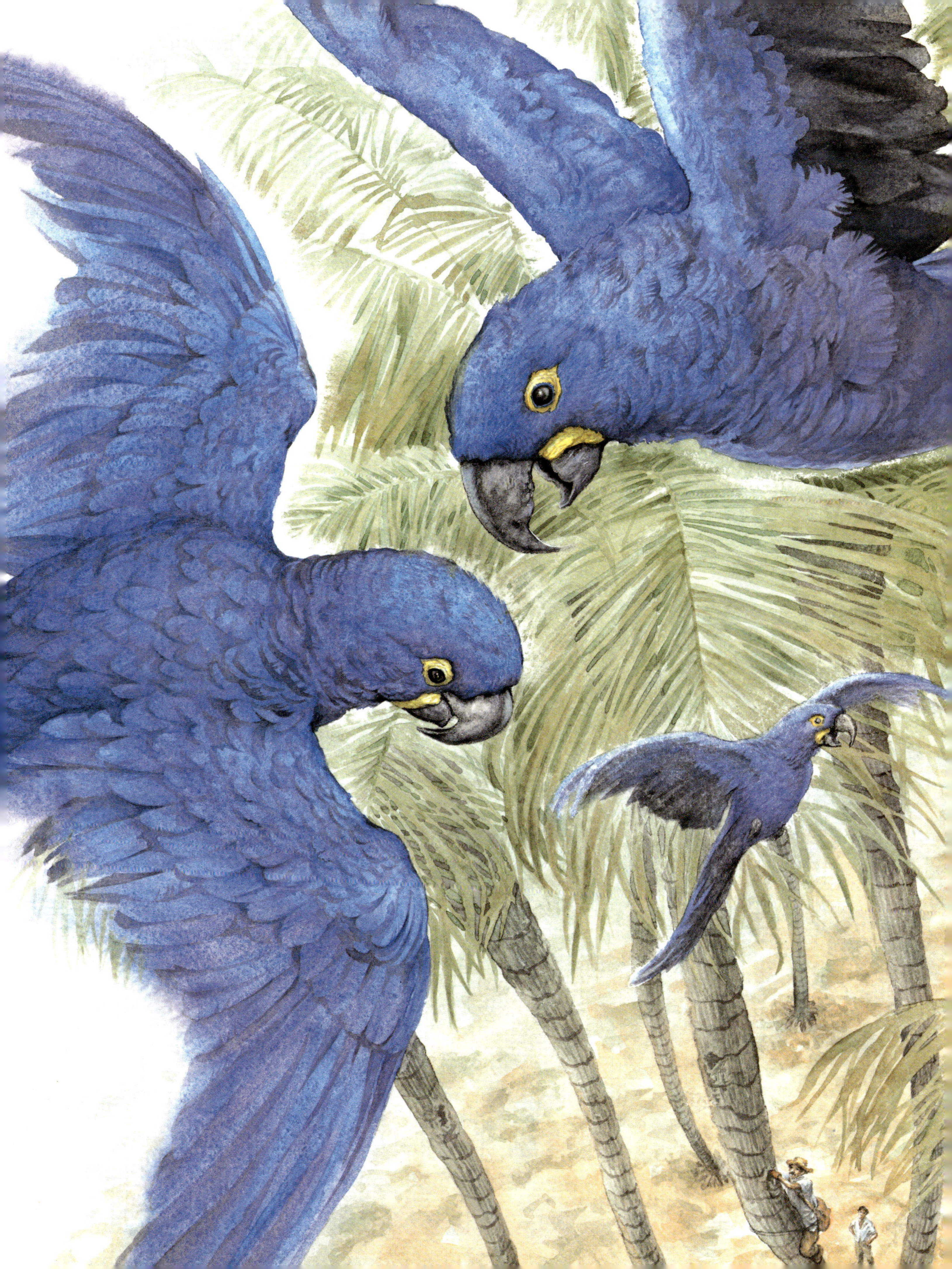

SOUTH AMERICA

Spectacled bear

The only bear in South America, this species takes its name from the white marks that ring its eyes. It dwells in wooded and open country high in the Andes Mountains, but is becoming increasingly scarce because these places are being cleared for farmland. It is also at risk because to find food it sometimes raids corn crops and attacks farm animals and farmers shoot it on sight.

FOUND IN:
Venezuela to Bolivia

SCIENTIFIC NAME:
Tremarctos ornatus

MAIN THREATS:
Hunting and habitat destruction

SIZE:
1.5–1.8 m long

Pampas deer

GRASSLAND AND MOUNTAIN ANIMALS

Hunting for sport, food and skins greatly reduced the numbers of pampas deer in South America. From 1860 to 1870, over two million skins were exported from Argentina alone. By 1975 that country had just 100 deer left. Today, with careful protection, there are now several hundred, but the deer will never recover fully because farms and cattle ranches have taken away the vast expanses of tall grass in which they once roamed.

FOUND IN:
Southern Brazil to northern Argentina

MAIN THREATS:
Hunting and habitat destruction

SCIENTIFIC NAME:
Ozotoceros bezoarticus

SIZE:
1–1.3 m long

Chaco tortoise

The Chaco tortoise roams across dry, thorny ground, chewing fruit, grass and cactus pads. Today it is in great peril because many thousands have been captured and smuggled abroad as pets, mainly to the United States. To save the wild population, the laws that are supposed to control this trade need to be enforced more strictly.

FOUND IN:
Paraguay and northern Argentina

MAIN THREATS:
Capture and hunting

SCIENTIFIC NAME:
Geochelone chilensis

SIZE:
Up to 36 cm long

Fluminense swallowtail

This beautiful butterfly is one of Brazil's most endangered insects. Drainage of its swampy, bushy habitat to build houses and factories and to lay out banana plantations has caused it to die out in many sites. Even the ten or so areas in which it still lives are under threat. Conservationists hope to be able to catch some butterflies and establish new colonies in safer places.

FOUND IN:
Southeastern Brazil

MAIN THREAT:
Habitat destruction

SCIENTIFIC NAME:
Parides ascanius

SIZE:
8 cm wingspan

SOUTH AMERICA

Northern screamer

FOUND IN:
Colombia and Venezuela

MAIN THREAT:
Hunting

SCIENTIFIC NAME:
Chauna chavaria

SIZE:
75–90 cm long

Although related to ducks and geese, the northern screamer does not have webbed feet like them and seldom swims in open water. This noisy bird is restricted to the rivers and swamps of a small area in the north of South America. Here it walks around over floating leaves, its long toes helping to spread its weight. Since it has a small population its survival is threatened by hunters who sometimes kill it for food.

Arrau river turtle

This turtle's habit of gathering in great numbers to lay its eggs on sandy riverbanks has led to its downfall. In the past, and still today, huge numbers of adults were killed and their eggs collected for food and oil. On some beaches, millions of eggs were stolen every year. Now a few of the beaches are protected and the eggs are placed in pens in which the young can hatch in safety.

FOUND IN:
Amazon and Orinoco river systems

MAIN THREAT:
Hunting

SCIENTIFIC NAME:
Podocnemis expansa

SIZE:
60–90 cm long

Spectacled caiman

FOUND IN:
Northern South America

MAIN THREAT:
Hunting

SCIENTIFIC NAME:
Caiman crocodilus

SIZE:
1.5–2.5 m long

FRESHWATER ANIMALS

Boto

This freshwater dolphin still swims in the Amazon and Orinoco rivers. However, the effects of dams which block the rivers, forest clearance on the banks, and pollution from pesticides and factory chemicals may all reduce the amount of fish it has to eat. Botos also get caught accidentally in fishing nets.

FOUND IN: **Amazon and Orinoco river systems**
MAIN THREATS: **Habitat disruption and pollution**
SCIENTIFIC NAME: *Inia geoffrensis*
SIZE: 2–3 m long

Pirarucu

The pirarucu is one of the biggest freshwater fish in the world. A fierce hunter, it cruises through shallow water looking for prey. It has become rare in many areas because of fishing for its flesh (sometimes rifles and even dynamite are used to kill it), and large numbers of young have been caught for the aquarium trade.

FOUND IN: **Amazon river system**
MAIN THREATS: **Overfishing and capture**
SCIENTIFIC NAME: *Arapaima gigas*
SIZE: Up to 3 m long

The fate of the spectacled caiman hangs on the changing demand for crocodile skin. Millions used to be killed for their hide every year, especially in Colombia and Peru where numbers have declined dramatically. Today, fashion has turned against this trade, but poaching of caimans still continues and could easily rise again if enough people want to buy crocodile skin products.

Africa

Two hundred years ago, Africa was teeming with wildlife. Today, many of its animals are at risk.

Africa's broad plains and dense forests were once full of wildlife. But when Europeans began to settle the continent in the nineteenth century, things started to change. More and more farms were built on the plains. Trees were cut down to make way for gardens and plantations. Before long, Africa's wildlife was in great danger.

The settlers' favourite sport was hunting. Soon they had killed millions of antelopes, zebras, giraffes, rhinoceroses, lions and leopards. Pushed from their old homes and hunted, African animals started to decrease in number.

Today the threats to wildlife are greater still. Africa's population is growing by more than twenty million people every year, most of whom are poor. They need more space for their farms, roads and settlements. There are too many cattle on the grasslands, and the forests are shrinking, but the deserts are growing. On the island of Madagascar, the forest is disappearing so fast that there may be almost none left in 30 years' time. Since most of Madagascar's animals live only in this forest, this would mean the extinction of hundreds of species.

Fortunately, Africa and Madagascar now have many reserves and national parks. Here some habitats are being preserved. Parks such as the Serengeti (Tanzania), Masai Mara (Kenya), Kruger (South Africa), Kafue (Zambia) and Tai (Ivory Coast) attract thousands of visitors every year.

The mountain gorilla has long been at risk from hunters who invade its misty highland home. Now it is strictly protected and tourists coming to see it in the wild help pay for its conservation.

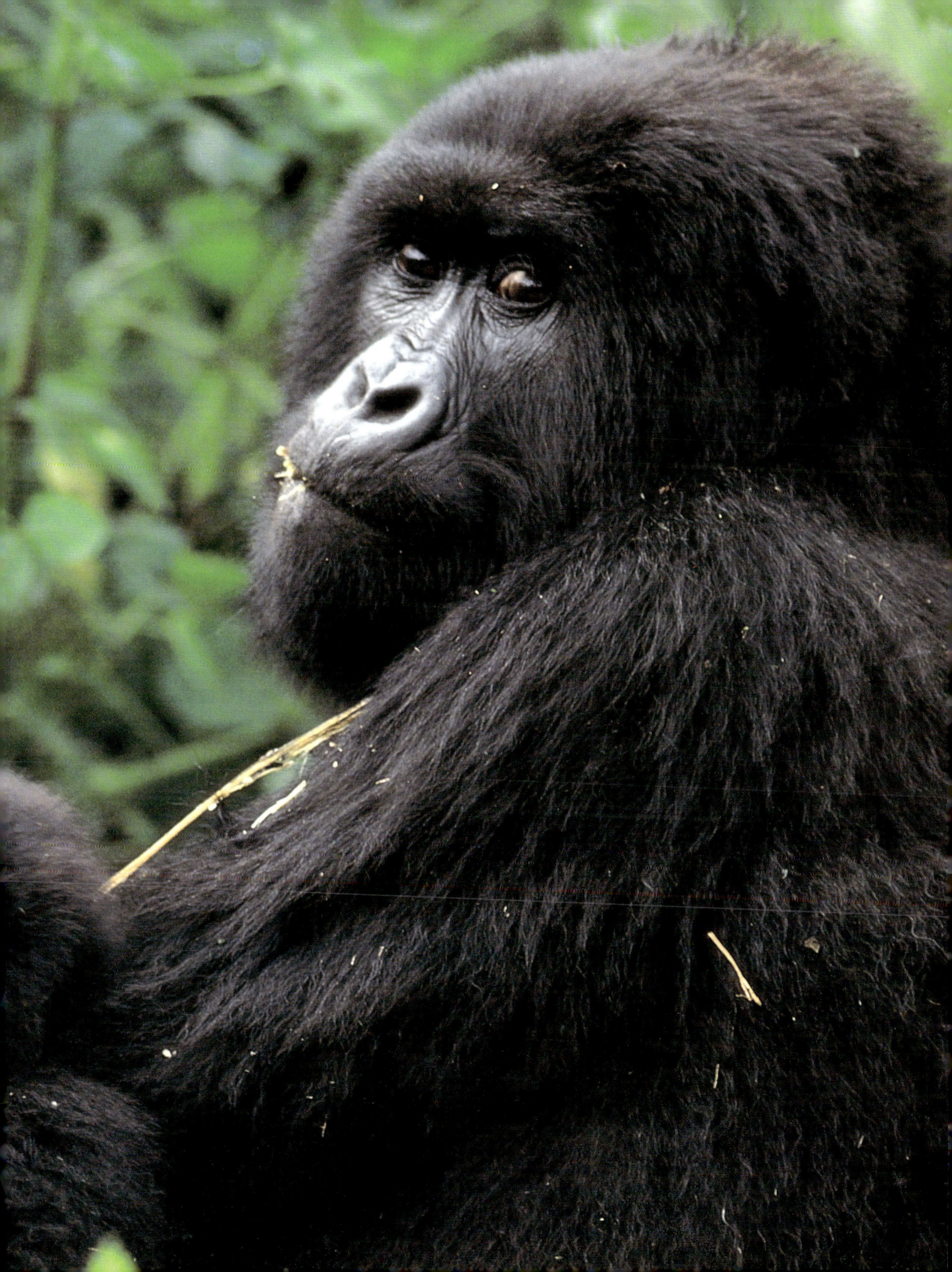

Africa's threatened animals

As Africa's human population grows and agricultural needs expand, its wildlife is gradually running out of space. Many of the wild grazing animals, for example, are being forced to leave the plains as cattle take over the pasture. Predatory animals such as the brown hyena may then try to catch livestock when they cannot find their natural prey. This puts them at risk from farmers. In southern Africa so many hyenas have been shot that they are now rarely seen outside reserves.

As with several unusual animals of South America's rainforests, many African animals are specifically adapted to a particular habitat and find survival difficult if their environment is disturbed. Huge areas of Africa's great rainforest have already been destroyed. This is a big threat to all the animals of the forest, especially to those that live in only a few areas. The white-necked rockfowl nests only in caves and on rocky cliffs surrounded by dense rainforest, but good sites are becoming hard to find. Madagascar's forests are being cleared so fast that 26 out of the 30 types of lemur on the island are threatened. This includes the indri, which is the biggest species.

① Barbary macaque

⑦ Bontebok

⑥ White-necked rockfowl

Africa

② Brown hyena

③ Nile crocodile

④ Indri

Hunting for food and poaching for skins, horns and tusks are great threats to animals already suffering because their habitats are being destroyed. From 1950 to 1980 at least three million Nile crocodiles were killed for their skins. Although in national parks the black rhinoceros is protected by armed guards, it is still not safe from poachers, who want its valuable horn. There are only a few thousand left in Africa.

The bontebok was ruthlessly hunted, but it was saved from extinction just in time. Reserves were created in the few areas of South Africa where it survived and the numbers of bontebok are growing again. There have also been projects to return some animals to the wild from captivity. Barbary macaques have been released in areas of north Africa where they once lived.

⑤ Black rhinoceros

43

Ruffed lemur

FOUND IN:
Eastern Madagascar

MAIN THREATS:
Habitat destruction, hunting and capture

SCIENTIFIC NAME:
Varecia variegata

SIZE:
Body 54–56 cm long, tail 58–65 cm

The ruffed lemur gets its name fron the thick collar of fur around its neck. In the lush rainforest of eastern Madagascar, where it makes its home, groups of up to five lemurs may be seen clambering through the trees in search of fruit. But their home is no longer safe. Large areas of the forest are being cut down for farmland. In addition, some people hunt lemurs for food, while others take them away as pets.

Congo peafowl

This shy, rare bird lives so deep in the African rainforest that scientists did not actually discover it until 1936 (they only knew it existed because a feather had been seen 23 years before). Even now, little is known about the Congo peafowl's life in the wild, but, because its numbers are already small, it is sure to suffer if more of the forest disappears.

FOUND IN:
Eastern Zaire

MAIN THREAT:
Habitat destruction

SCIENTIFIC NAME:
Afropavo congensis

SIZE:
60–70 cm long

FOUND IN:
West Africa

MAIN THREATS:
Habitat destruction and hunting

SCIENTIFIC NAME:
Choeropsis liberiensis

SIZE:
1.8–2.1 m long

RAINFOREST ANIMALS

Chimpanzee

There are fewer than 200,000 chimpanzees left in the wild. This sounds like a lot, but they are scattered over a large area and have disappeared from many places where their habitat has been destroyed. Hunting chimpanzees is against the law now but it still goes on. Some people kill the adults so that they can capture the young ones to sell abroad for medical experiments.

FOUND IN:
West and Central Africa

SCIENTIFIC NAME:
Pan troglodytes

MAIN THREATS:
Habitat destruction, hunting and capture

SIZE:
64–94 cm long

Aye-aye

FOUND IN:
Madagascar

SCIENTIFIC NAME:
Daubentonia madagascariensis

MAIN THREATS:
Habitat destruction and hunting

SIZE:
Body 36–44 cm long, tail 50–60 cm

The aye-aye uses its very long middle finger to pull insects out of tree bark. Local tradition says that this strange animal brings bad luck and for that reason it is often killed. Conservationists hope they can change these old beliefs and make people want to protect both the aye-aye and its forest home.

Pygmy hippopotamus

This small cousin of the well-known hippopotamus often lives around swamps, but it spends most of its time on dry land. It has become rare in all the places where it still lives. Most of its forest habitat has already been cut down and hunters kill the animal for its meat. Conservationists say that its numbers will fall dramatically unless it is given careful protection inside nature reserves.

Focus on: African elephant

The African elephant is one of the best loved of all animals, but this has not saved it from the hunter's gun. The elephant is at risk because of its ivory tusks. This ivory used to be sent all over the world and made into things like piano keys, carvings and jewellery. Eventually laws were passed to control hunting. But ivory is now so valuable that poachers ignore the law and even go deep into nature reserves in search of elephants to kill. During the 1980s the number of wild elephants in all of Africa crashed faster than ever, from 1.3 million in 1979 down to 600,000 by 1990.

Only drastic action could save the elephant, so in 1989 most countries agreed to ban all trade in ivory. Poaching declined after this. Now some African countries want to start selling ivory legally again, but a lot of other countries would like to keep the ban until the elephant population has had a better chance to recover.

Dustbathing in safety
In well-guarded reserves there is much less poaching and elephant herds are fairly safe. A few reserves in southern Africa are even said to be overcrowded with elephants.

Prey to the gun
Gangs of elephant poachers are armed with rifles and machine guns. When they find a herd, they shoot as many as they can, then cut off all the ivory tusks. In the 1980s about 1,500 elephants were killed every week. Since the ban on ivory trading in 1989, the number killed by poachers has dropped in most areas.

Burning tusks
These tusks, worth millions of dollars, have been seized from poachers. By burning them, the Kenyan government has made sure they will not be sold or smuggled to ivory carvers in Asia. If shops stop buying ivory items, the elephants will be helped even more.

Hermit ibis

This peculiar bald-headed bird used to be much more widespread, but it does not cope well with changes in its habitat and food supply caused by farming. Last seen in Turkey in 1989, it now breeds only in Morocco, in a rather dry, rocky area where there is not much farming. Although the four nesting colonies there have increased slightly in size, the total wild population of 220 is still small.

FOUND IN: **Morocco**
MAIN THREAT: **Habitat destruction**
SCIENTIFIC NAME: *Geronticus eremita*
SIZE: **71–79 cm long**

African pancake tortoise

This remarkable tortoise has a soft, flexible shell. If in danger, it can crawl into a rocky crevice and breathe in lots of air, making its body expand so much that it is stuck fast and very difficult to pull out. But this does not protect the animal from hunters who catch large numbers for the pet trade.

FOUND IN: **Kenya and Tanzania**
MAIN THREAT: **Capture**
SCIENTIFIC NAME: *Malocochersus tornieri*
SIZE: **17 cm long**

Addax

The addax is one of the few large animals that live in the Sahara Desert. It feeds on desert plants and gets all the moisture it needs from them. It has been hunted near to extinction for sport and for its horns, and where it still lives cattle often trample on and destroy its food. Plans to release some captive addax into reserves may succeed, but only if people leave them in peace.

GRASSLAND AND DESERT ANIMALS

Grevy's zebra

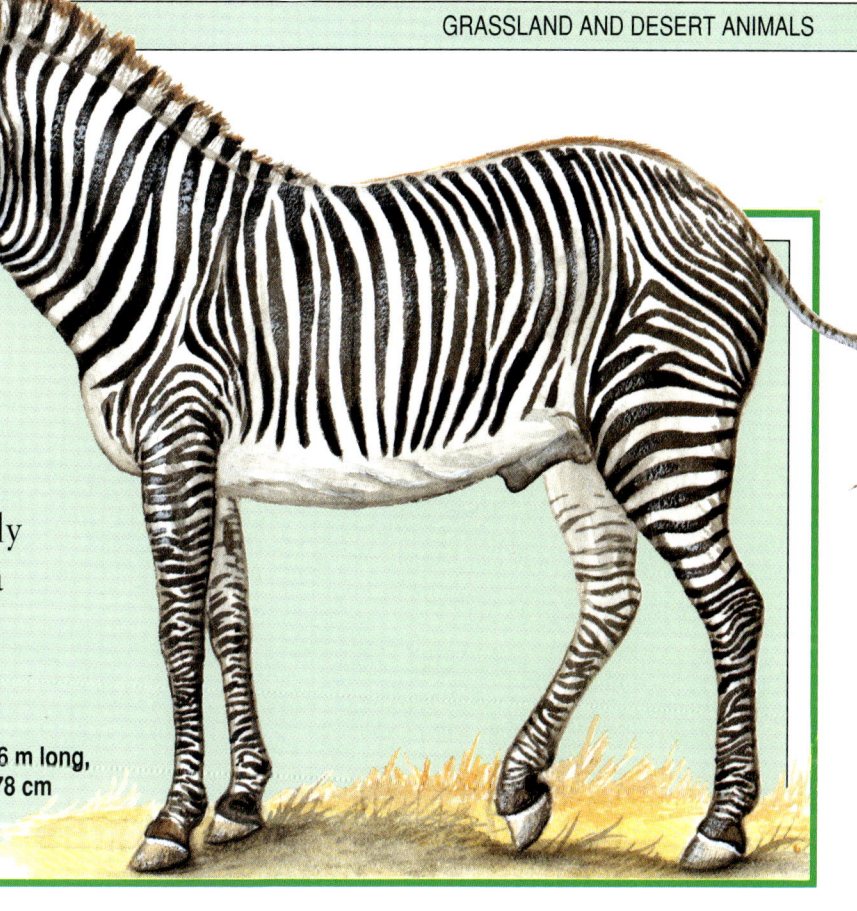

Grevy's zebra is endangered because its beautiful, narrow-striped coat makes the animal a target for hunters who sell skins. The largest of all zebras, it roams across dry, sparsely wooded country from northern Kenya to Ethiopia. There are probably now no more than 15,000 animals left.

FOUND IN: **East Africa**

MAIN THREATS: **Hunting and habitat destruction**

SCIENTIFIC NAME: *Equus grevyi*

SIZE: **Body 2.6 m long, tail 75–78 cm**

FOUND IN: **North Africa**

SCIENTIFIC NAME: *Addax nasomaculatus*

MAIN THREATS: **Hunting and habitat destruction**

SIZE: **Body 1.3 m long, tail 25–35 cm**

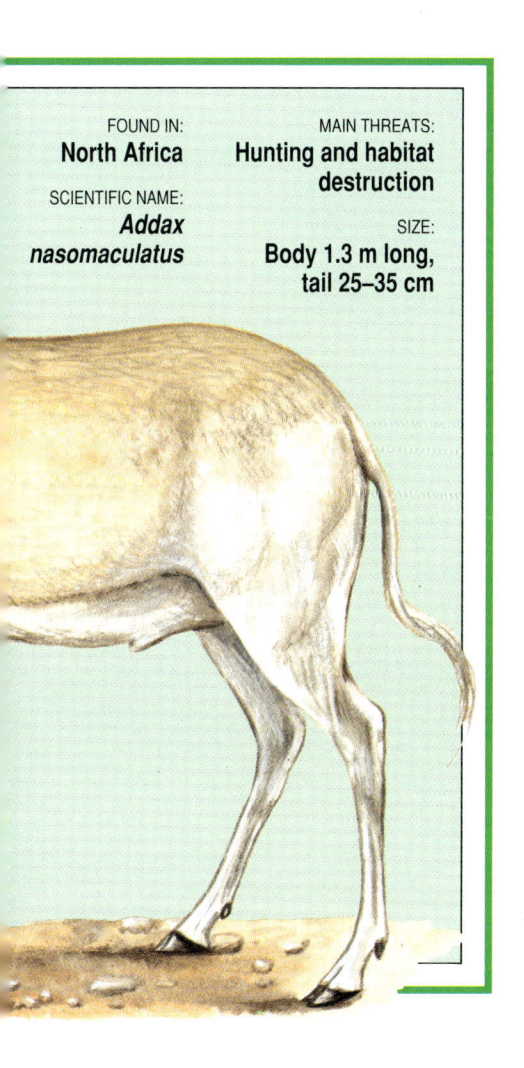

Hunting dog

Hunting dogs once stalked prey throughout the African savanna, but today they are found only in a few scattered places. Huge numbers of the dogs have been shot by farmers who believe they will attack their livestock. To survive the dogs need large, wild areas of land with plenty of prey such as zebra. Today, most places like this are in national parks.

FOUND IN: **Africa, south of the Sahara**

MAIN THREATS: **Hunting and habitat destruction**

SCIENTIFIC NAME: *Lycaon pictus*

SIZE: **Body up to 1.1 m long, tail 30–40 cm**

AFRICA

Madagascar fish eagle

With only about 30 nesting pairs left, this is one of the rarest of all birds. In the 1930s it was still quite common along the northwest coast of Madagascar, but since then it has declined dramatically, partly because it has been shot and its nests destroyed. It usually hunts around estuaries and coastal swamps where it can plunge down to catch fish.

FOUND IN:	MAIN THREATS:	SCIENTIFIC NAME:	SIZE:
Northwest Madagascar	Hunting and disturbance	*Haliaeetus vociferoides*	70–80 cm long

West African dwarf crocodile

This small crocodile has become rare in recent years because of changes to the rivers and lakes it inhabits and because of ruthless hunting. A slow-moving and not very dangerous animal, it is easy to kill or catch. Some people take it for its meat, but most want to sell its skin for money. There are even whole, stuffed animals on sale to tourists in some countries.

FOUND IN:	MAIN THREATS:	SCIENTIFIC NAME:	SIZE:
West and Central Africa	Hunting and habitat disruption	*Osteolaemus tetraspis*	1.5 m long

FRESHWATER AND SEA ANIMALS

Coelacanth

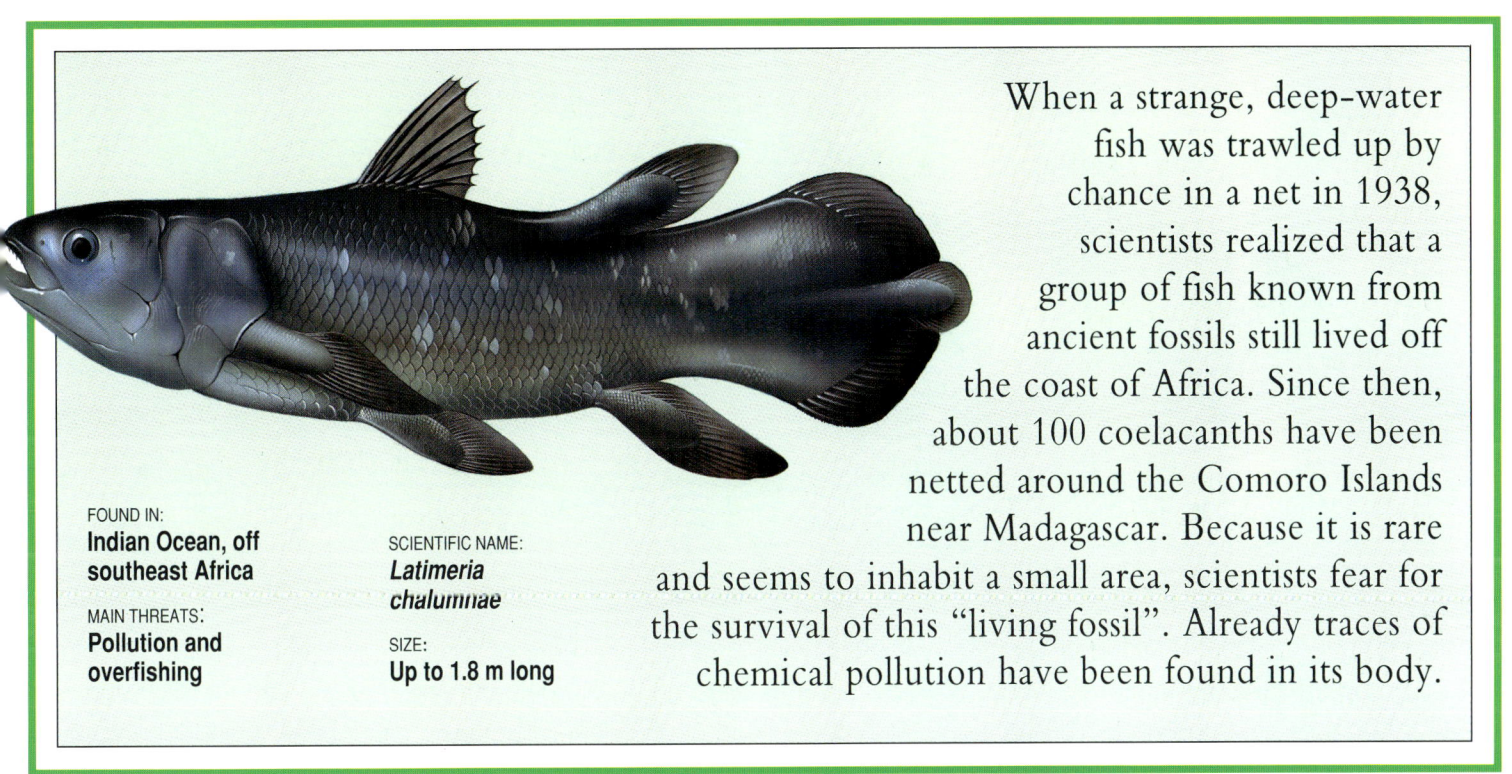

When a strange, deep-water fish was trawled up by chance in a net in 1938, scientists realized that a group of fish known from ancient fossils still lived off the coast of Africa. Since then, about 100 coelacanths have been netted around the Comoro Islands near Madagascar. Because it is rare and seems to inhabit a small area, scientists fear for the survival of this "living fossil". Already traces of chemical pollution have been found in its body.

FOUND IN:
Indian Ocean, off southeast Africa

MAIN THREATS:
Pollution and overfishing

SCIENTIFIC NAME:
Latimeria chalumnae

SIZE:
Up to 1.8 m long

Allen's swamp monkey

This little-known monkey lives alongside rivers and in swamps. Though it eats mainly leaves and fruit, it also goes into the water to snatch crabs and even fish. It, in turn, is hunted by local people for meat and because it sometimes raids farmers' crops. Because it prefers waterside trees, the monkey is quite easy for hunters in boats to track down and shoot.

FOUND IN:
Congo and Zaire

SCIENTIFIC NAME:
Allenopithecus nigroviridis

SIZE:
Body 40–50 cm long, tail 45–55 cm

MAIN THREAT:
Hunting

Europe

In Europe's crowded landscape, any small area of unpolluted land has become a precious refuge for wildlife.

Europe was once almost completely covered by thick woodland. Today, the continent is crowded with people, farms, settlements and roads; natural habitats are like islands in a sea of towns and cities. Animals that used to roam widely, such as bears, wild boars, wolves, storks and eagles, have disappeared from most regions.

New opportunities for wildlife have been created—hedgerows, grazing meadows and grouse moors are artificial habitats that have become homes to certain species. However, many of these habitats are now threatened as farmers try to make their land more productive.

Europe's concentration of people, farmland and industry brings other problems. Heavy pollution harms river and sea creatures. It also affects animals that feed on these creatures, such as the otter and the osprey. More than half the Mediterranean coastline is polluted by sewage. Hunters still threaten many animals: every year a total of 900 million birds are killed for sport as they migrate between Europe and Africa.

Fortunately, conservation efforts have helped many European animals. There are strong laws to protect wildlife and increasing controls on pollution. Each country has reserves and parks for wildlife. These protect areas of undamaged land and those that have been least disturbed by people, such as mountains and wetlands.

The large copper butterfly lives in fens and marshes—wetland areas that are becoming increasingly scarce because of land drainage for farming. This butterfly is extinct in Britain and rare all over Europe.

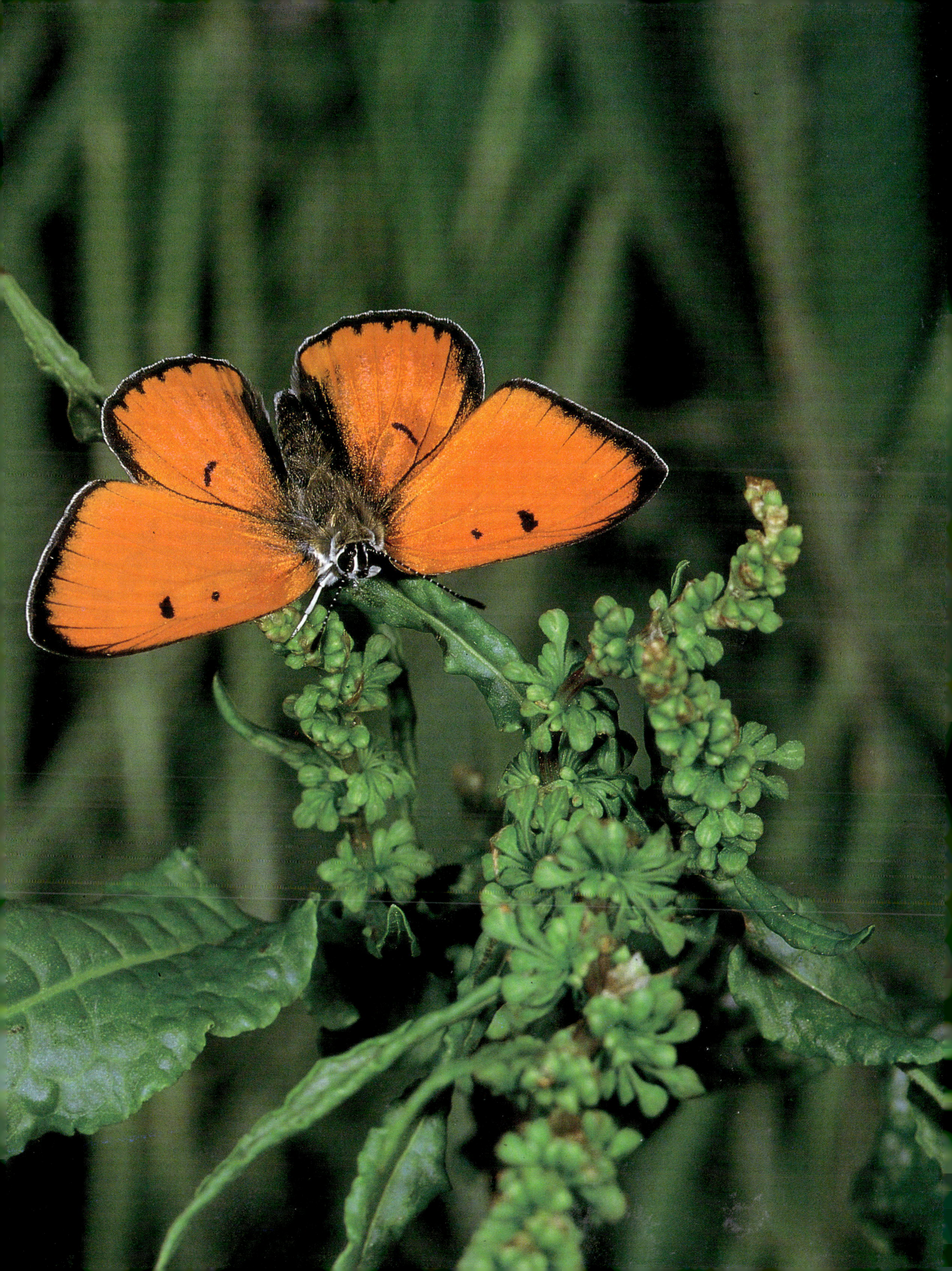

Europe's threatened animals

All sorts of problems threaten wildlife across densely populated Europe. The barn owl has been hunted so much by gamekeepers and sportsmen that it became scarce in Europe over 100 years ago. Since then, many of the old trees and barns in which it nested have been removed. The owl is also poisoned by pesticides and is often killed by road traffic. In some countries there are only a few hundred pairs of barn owls left.

Similarly, the rare Russian desman was widely hunted in the rivers of western Russia for its soft fur. The desman has also had to cope with increasing water pollution, changing river levels and invasion of its habitat by muskrats and coypus that have escaped from farms where they are bred for their fur. These animals compete with the desman for space and food. The starlet sea anemone, which lives in tidal pools, has also suffered from pollution. It survives at just four places in southern England.

Some animals such as the hobby are still trying to recover from the time when hunting was most popular in the nineteenth century. During that time the hobby became very rare, mainly because gamekeepers killed it and egg-collectors raided its nests. Today it is still scarce, even in

① Russian desman

⑥ Hobby

Europe

② Wild cat

③ Barn owl

places where hunting has stopped. The bowhead whale, which swims in the cold waters of the Arctic Ocean, was hunted almost to extinction by whalers. A slow mover, it was easier to catch than other whales, and because of its large size it also yielded plenty of whalebone and oil. Whalers stopped hunting this giant animal long ago, but there are few in the seas near Europe.

The loggerhead turtle, which lives in the Mediterranean Sea, has suffered because hotels and tourists have spoiled most of the beaches on which it used to lay its eggs. However, many people are now campaigning to save the turtle and parts of some beaches have been made into turtle sanctuaries.

Changing attitudes toward wildlife have already helped lots of animals in Europe. The wild cat was ruthlessly hunted in the past to protect game such as grouse and partridges, but far fewer people want to shoot or trap it today. As a result, the wild cat has increased in numbers and is returning to some of the forests and moors where it used to live.

④ Loggerhead turtle

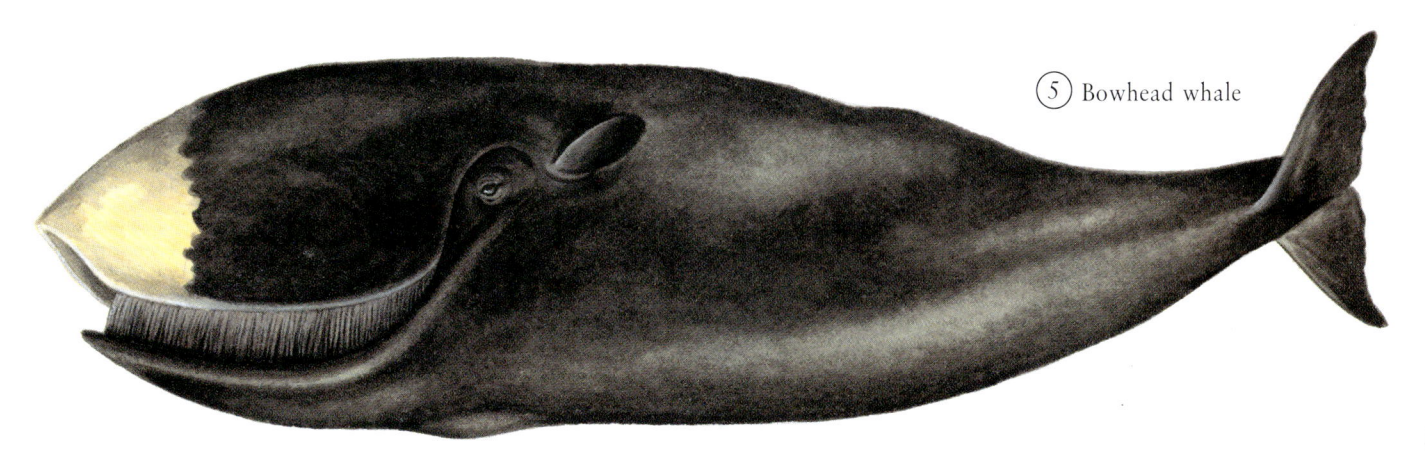

⑤ Bowhead whale

55

EUROPE

Corncrake

FOUND IN:
Europe and western Asia

MAIN THREATS:
Habitat destruction and disturbance

SCIENTIFIC NAME:
Crex crex

SIZE:
25–30 cm long

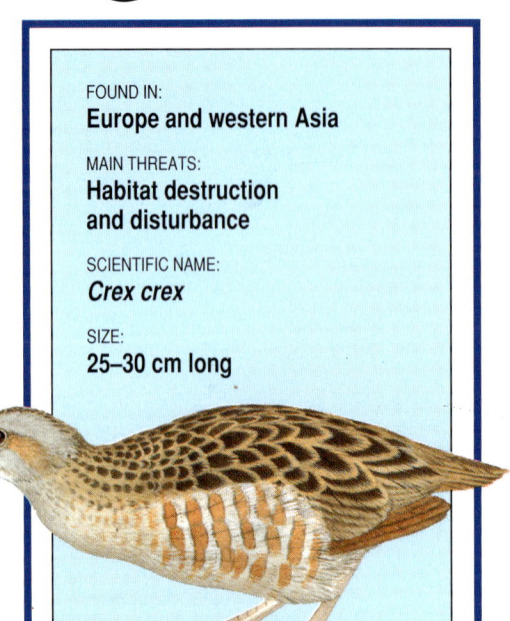

The corncrake used to thrive on farms, often nesting in the hayfields, but farms are now dangerous places to live. As more and more hedgerows are removed, weeds killed and field edges tidied, the birds have fewer places to hide and find food. Haycutting machines ruin many nests and even kill adults and chicks. The corncrake is becoming rare in most countries.

Greater horseshoe bat

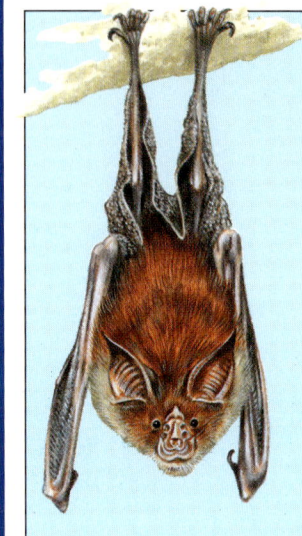

This bat roosts inside caves, hollow trees and roofs. But as caves are explored, trees felled and old buildings pulled down, homes are becoming harder to find. Many bats have been poisoned by chemicals used to preserve roof timber. The species is almost extinct in northwestern Europe.

FOUND IN:
Europe, Asia and North Africa

MAIN THREATS:
Habitat destruction, disturbance and poisoning

SCIENTIFIC NAME:
Rhinolophus ferrumequinum

SIZE:
5.5–7 cm long

Spur-thighed tortoise

This tortoise comes from dry, scrubby regions around the Mediterranean Sea—places that are being changed by farming and the building of holiday homes. It is rare because millions were captured and sold as pets. Some trade still goes on, but it is now banned by most countries to give the tortoises a chance to recover in the wild.

FOUND IN:
Southern Europe and North Africa

MAIN THREATS:
Capture and habitat destruction

SCIENTIFIC NAME:
Testudo graeca

SIZE:
Up to 25 cm long

GRASSLAND AND WOODLAND ANIMALS

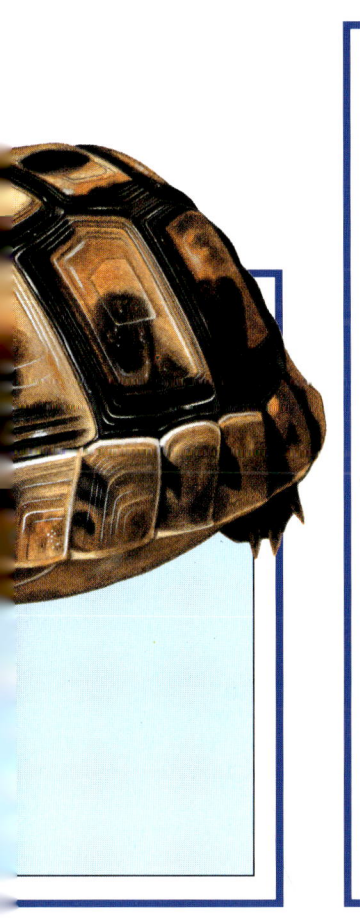

European bison

Like its American cousin, the European bison was hunted for its meat. Although it died out in the wild in 1919, there were still some animals in zoos. Six of these were set free in a safe part of Poland's Bialowieza forest. They bred and prospered, and now more than 250 bison live wild in the forest again.

FOUND IN:	MAIN THREAT:	SCIENTIFIC NAME:	SIZE:
Eastern Europe	Hunting	*Bison bonasus*	2.5–2.7 m long

Red kite

FOUND IN:
Western, southern and eastern Europe

MAIN THREATS:
Hunting and capture

SCIENTIFIC NAME:
Milvus milvus

SIZE:
61–66 cm long

The red kite was a common scavenger hundreds of years ago, before hunters destroyed huge numbers. Now, fewer than fifty pairs survive in most countries, and it is rare enough for people to make money by stealing its eggs and young to sell. And illegal killing still goes on: in 1989, eleven kites were found poisoned in Wales, their only British nesting site.

Focus on: European otter

The otter has become rare in many parts of Europe, especially in lowland areas which have the most people, towns, farms and factories. The worst problem it faces is pollution of the rivers, lakes and marshes in which it hunts for fish and other water creatures. The first sign of this came in the 1950s when otters declined rapidly in Britain. Studies showed they had been poisoned by powerful chemicals called organochlorine pesticides that farmers were putting in sheep dips and spraying on their crops. These washed into streams and passed to the otters through their food.

Most farmers stopped using these pesticides, but other kinds of pollution, including factory waste, continued to ruin rivers. Otters now no longer live in Switzerland, for example, because the rivers have been badly contaminated. Fortunately, lots of people want to save the otter. They hope that if rivers can be cleaned up and otter habitats conserved, the animal will one day return to some of its old homes.

The perils of dirty water
Otters are very sensitive to pollution. If they eat lots of fish that have been feeding in polluted rivers and lakes, dangerous chemicals quickly build up in their own bodies. Sometimes the otters eat so much polluted fish that they are poisoned to death. Or the chemicals they consume may make them unable or too unhealthy to breed. If the adults are no longer producing young, the otter population in a polluted area is doomed to die out.

Ideal home
Otters like rivers with plenty of plants growing on the banks and mature overhanging trees under which they can make their dens. Sadly, many riversides in lowland Europe have been cleared and old trees have been chopped down. Helping otters to survive can include replanting trees along riverbanks and providing artificial dens made from rocks or sticks.

Dalmatian pelican

FOUND IN:
Southeastern Europe to China

SCIENTIFIC NAME:
Pelecanus crispus

MAIN THREATS:
Habitat destruction and hunting

SIZE:
Up to 1.8 m long

With the perfect bill for scooping up fish, it is not surprising that the Dalmatian pelican is the enemy of many fish-farmers. But because fish-farmers and fishermen shoot so many pelicans and because marshy habitats are being drained, farmed or built over, this bird is now very rare. Millions of pelicans used to nest on the delta of the river Danube—now there are just 40 pairs there.

Medicinal leech

FOUND IN:
Western, southern and eastern Europe

SCIENTIFIC NAME:
Hirudo medicinalis

MAIN THREAT:
Capture

SIZE:
10–12.5 cm long

In the nineteenth century, many doctors used leeches to remove blood from their patients as a way of treating some illnesses. Leeches normally suck blood from animals that wade into streams or ponds. Millions of them were taken from the wild every year, and they soon became scarce. Today, leeches are in demand again for the special substance they have that stops blood clotting.

FOUND IN:
Mediterranean Sea

MAIN THREATS:
Pollution and hunting

SCIENTIFIC NAME:
Monachus monachus

SIZE:
2–3.1 m long

FOUND IN:
European coastal waters

SCIENTIFIC NAME:
Acipenser sturio

MAIN THREATS:
Overfishing and habitat disruption

SIZE:
1–3 m long

Mediterranean monk seal

There are probably fewer than 500 of these seals left in the entire Mediterranean. They are still hunted by fishermen who blame them for tearing open nets and snatching captured fish. Most of the seal colonies that have survived now live in caves. These caves often have underwater entrances, which are difficult to enter.

Common sturgeon

The common sturgeon spends most of its time foraging on the seabed, but every year it swims up to 500 km inland to spawn. But dams and other obstructions have stopped it breeding in many rivers, and at sea huge numbers have been caught for food. A famous and expensive food called caviar is made of eggs taken from the female fish. Today, the sturgeon is scarce in most waters.

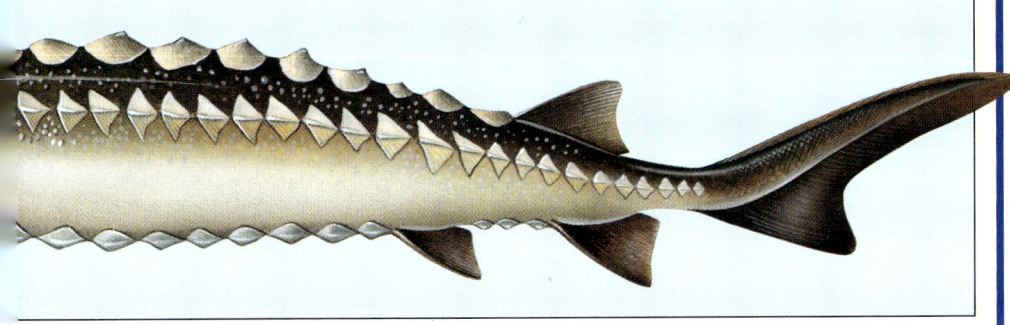

Olm

This strange salamander lives in the darkness of underground streams and lakes. There it rummages in the mud to find food. Animal collectors have taken so many of these fascinating creatures from the wild that new areas where they have been found are kept secret. Conservationists are also worried that the clean water in which they swim may become polluted by factories.

FOUND IN:
Yugoslavia and Italy

SCIENTIFIC NAME:
Proteus anguinus

MAIN THREATS:
Capture and pollution

SIZE:
20–30 cm long

Asia

Ruthless hunting and the destruction of natural habitats have put many of Asia's animals in danger.

With its huge size, varied landscape and uneven spread of people, Asia poses different problems for wildlife in different regions. In the north and west, where few people live, many wild places for animals remain. However, hunting has endangered some larger creatures such as antelopes, deer and big cats.

By contrast, in the crowded lands of the south and east cultivation has changed much of the landscape. Grasslands have been thinned and large areas of forest have been cleared. In these parts, many animals now only survive in protected areas. Even when animals are officially protected they are not always safe. Poachers have continued to shoot Asian elephants even though they live inside Thailand's Khao Yai National Park.

There are still large areas of tropical rainforest across the islands of Southeast Asia. But every year the increase in population and the actions of logging companies reduce the rainforest. At least 126 species of birds in Indonesia are endangered—the highest number for any country in the world.

Efforts are now being made to help the animals at risk. Animals are protected in national parks and reserves and by the work of environmentalists. The Chikpo protest movement in India has managed to stop some logging plans, for example. Meanwhile, conservation programmes have saved animals such as the Arabian oryx from the brink of extinction.

Ten years after hunters killed the last wild Arabian oryx, the animals reappeared in the desert. Groups of oryx from zoos were carefully brought back to the wild and there are now about 100 roaming free.

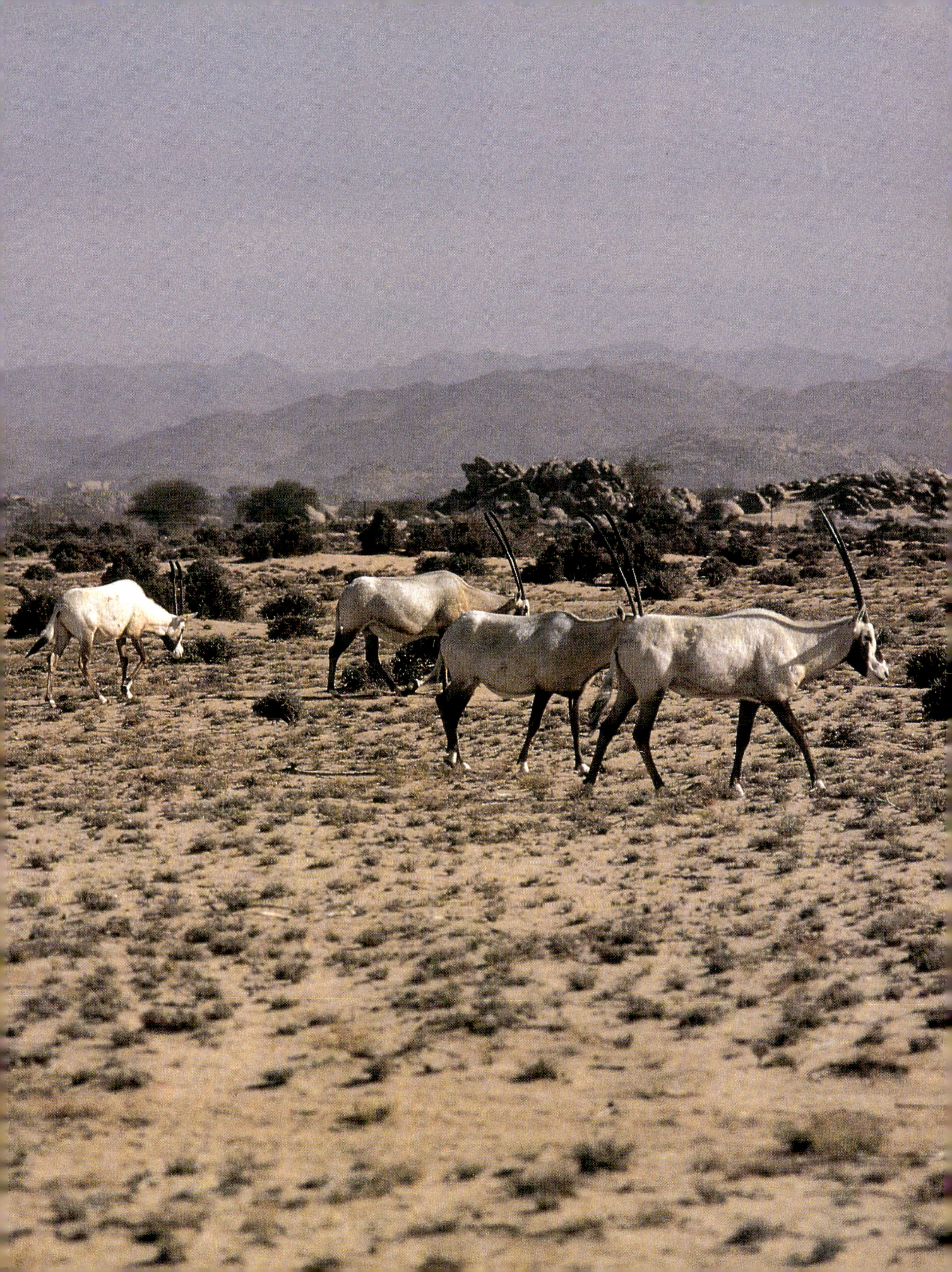

Asia's threatened animals

The gradual spread of farms and settlements into wild habitats is the biggest problem for wildlife in Asia. It threatens some famous endangered animals. The giant panda, the symbol of the World Wide Fund for Nature, has lost most of the Chinese bamboo forests it inhabits. Now fewer than 1,000 pandas remain, scattered in small groups. The tiger has disappeared from many parts of south and east Asia. It needs a large area of forest in which to hunt, and quickly runs out of space if burning and felling damage its home. From 6,000 to 9,000 wild tigers are left—in 1900 India alone had 50,000. Another big mammal, the leaf-eating Malayan tapir, is in great danger because of deforestation in Malaya and Sumatra.

Hunting, too, takes its toll on these animals. Poachers kill pandas and tigers to sell their valuable skins. Farmers shoot tapirs if they come out of the forest to raid crops. Hunting also threatens the Victoria crowned pigeon. At up to 85 cm in length, it is a giant among pigeons, and it provides plenty of tasty meat for people in the forests of New Guinea. The Indian python is a big, powerful snake, capable of

① Indian python

⑥ Siberian white crane

⑦ Onager

Asia

② Tiger

suffocating a leopard in its coils. But it, too, has disappeared from many regions—it is hunted for its skin and captured for the pet trade.

In recent years there have been big efforts to conserve some of these spectacular animals. The Chinese government has promised to fund lots of new reserves for pandas. Tigers have more than doubled in number in India since 1970, helped by special refuges such as the Ranthambore Tiger Reserve. The onager, a type of wild ass from Iran and Turkmenistan, was hunted and pushed from good pasture and drinking water by farmers' herds. But its numbers are rising again and some animals that were raised in captivity have been released back into the wild.

The wild population of the rare Siberian white crane is just 14. Conservationists hope to increase the number by fooling other nesting cranes into acting as foster parents for the white crane's eggs. Some of the eggs they plan to use will have been laid by captive white cranes in the United States.

③ Giant panda

⑤ Victoria crowned pigeon

④ Malayan tapir

ASIA

Pileated gibbon

The pileated gibbon uses its long arms to swing from branch to branch, high in forest trees. Tree clearing has taken away most of the mature forest it needs, and local people kill the animal for its meat. Once there were two to three million gibbons in Thailand alone; now the total population is probably below 20,000.

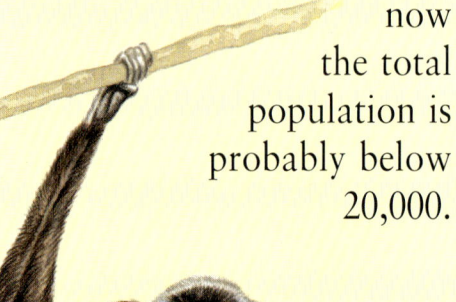

FOUND IN:
Thailand, Cambodia and Laos

MAIN THREATS:
Habitat destruction and hunting

SCIENTIFIC NAME:
Hylobates pileatus

SIZE:
47-60 cm long

Helmeted hornbill

The thick lump on the helmeted hornbill's beak is made of solid ivory and is more valuable than elephant ivory. Ivory hunters have caused the bird to disappear from many areas. It is also badly affected by tree felling because each pair of birds needs a large area of forest in which to find food.

FOUND IN:
Malaysia, Borneo and Sumatra

MAIN THREATS:
Hunting and habitat destruction

SCIENTIFIC NAME:
Rhinoplax vigil

SIZE:
Body up to 70 cm long, tail up to 50 cm

Sumatran rhinoceros

This is the smallest and hairiest of all the rhinoceroses. Its horn, which is ground to powder and used in traditional medicine, is very valuable and much sought after. There are now only a few hundred left and many of the forests in which they survive are being chopped down. This leaves small groups of rhinos marooned and even more at risk from poachers.

Queen Alexandra's birdwing

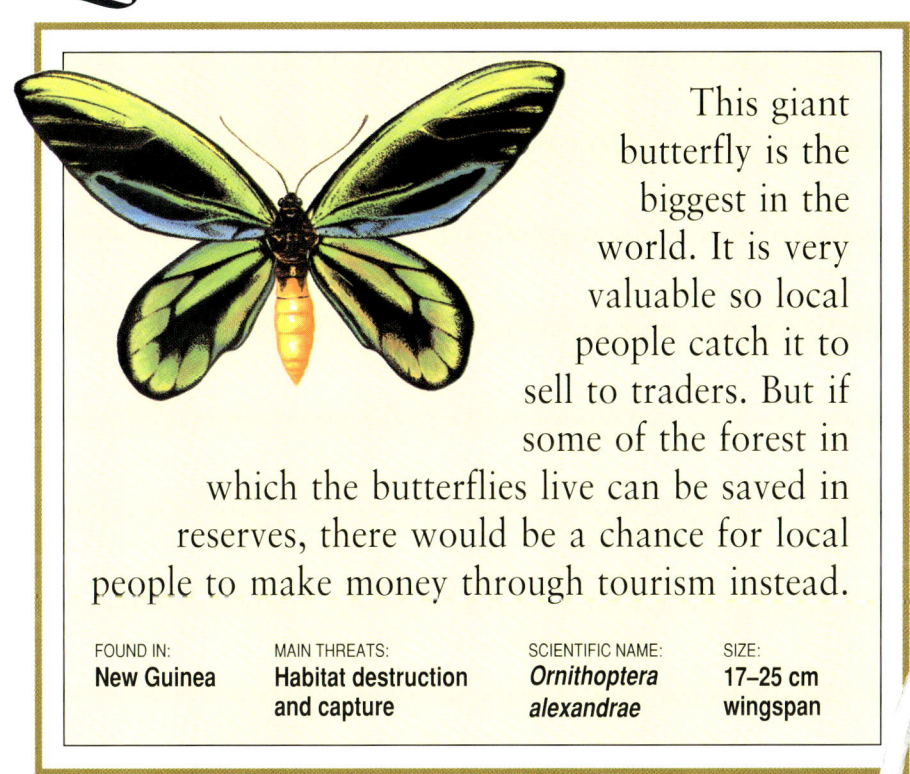

This giant butterfly is the biggest in the world. It is very valuable so local people catch it to sell to traders. But if some of the forest in which the butterflies live can be saved in reserves, there would be a chance for local people to make money through tourism instead.

FOUND IN:
New Guinea

MAIN THREATS:
Habitat destruction and capture

SCIENTIFIC NAME:
Ornithoptera alexandrae

SIZE:
17–25 cm wingspan

FOUND IN:
Southeast Asia

MAIN THREATS:
Hunting and habitat destruction

SCIENTIFIC NAME:
Dicerorhinus sumatrensis

SIZE:
2.5–2.8 m long

Ribbon-tailed bird of paradise

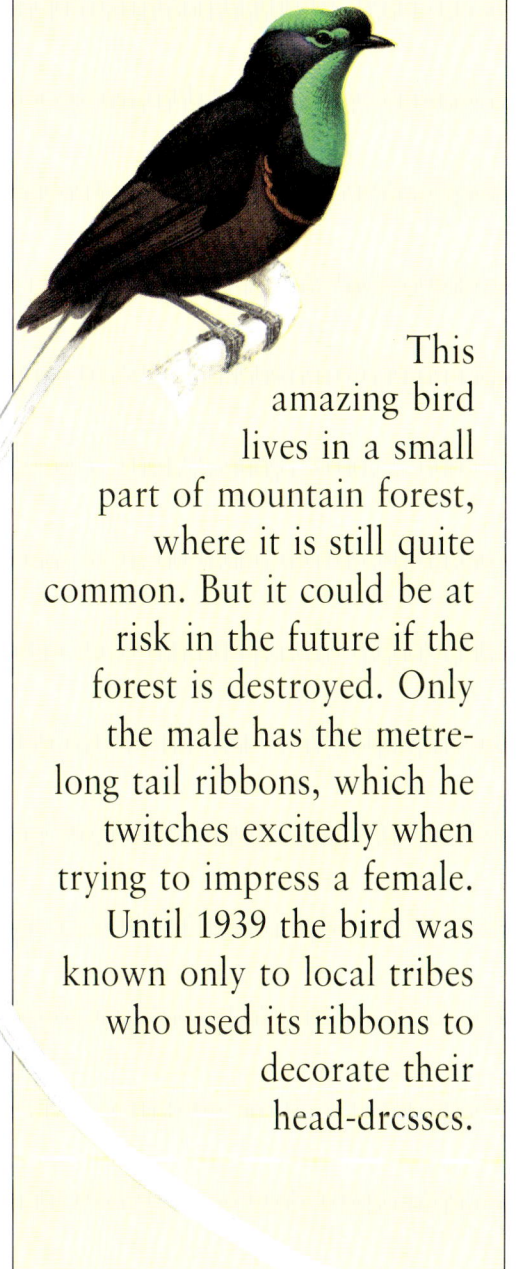

This amazing bird lives in a small part of mountain forest, where it is still quite common. But it could be at risk in the future if the forest is destroyed. Only the male has the metre-long tail ribbons, which he twitches excitedly when trying to impress a female. Until 1939 the bird was known only to local tribes who used its ribbons to decorate their head-dresses.

FOUND IN:
New Guinea

MAIN THREATS:
Hunting and habitat destruction

SCIENTIFIC NAME:
Astrapia mayeri

SIZE:
Body 30–35 cm long, tail streamers up to 1 m

Focus on: Orangutan

Nobody knows exactly how many orangutans there are living deep in the tropical rainforests of Sumatra and Borneo, but the number could now be as low as a few thousand. Every year, more and more of their forest home is cut down, mainly for timber. The shy orangutan cannot survive even selective logging, in which only the biggest trees are removed, because it can no longer move about easily from branch to branch in the forest canopy and find enough food.

Once tree felling begins, an orangutan will hide in another patch of forest. But the new area will be unfamiliar and the wandering ape may find itself trespassing in a neighbour's patch (each orangutan needs as much as five square kilometres of forest to live in). The newcomer may not be able to find enough food. Also, it is unlikely to breed if it cannot find enough space to live in. Some young orangutans are also captured and traded illegally as pets or laboratory animals for medical experiments.

Home from home
At forest sanctuaries such as the Sepilok Rehabilitation Centre in Borneo, once-captive orangutans are given the chance to return to the wild. Many of these apes have been taken back from people trying to smuggle them overseas for sale. They are often in poor condition and need careful tending before they can be released back into the surrounding forest.

Fallen giants
Logging of rainforest trees for timber poses a huge threat not just to orangutans but to all the wildlife in Southeast Asian rainforests. Sumatra has already lost more than half its forests and logging even threatens some nature reserves.

Life in the trees
Orangutans spend most of their lives high in the rainforest canopy. They swing from branch to branch to feed on fruit by day and rest on nests of broken branches and leaves by night. Logging quickly ruins their home. It opens up gaps in the canopy, breaks the dangling creepers they use for climbing and destroys necessary food plants such as creeping figs.

ASIA

Snow leopard

There might be 5,000 snow leopards still living in the high mountains of central Asia. Although their home is so remote, the leopards are still persecuted by hunters who shoot them for their beautiful fur, which is very valuable. Farmers also shoot them because they sometimes attack herds when they cannot find their normal prey—wild goats.

FOUND IN:
Central Asia

MAIN THREAT:
Hunting

SCIENTIFIC NAME:
Panthera uncia

SIZE:
Body 1.2–1.5 m long, tail 90 cm–1.1 m

Cheer pheasant

The cheer pheasant lives on steep, grassy slopes up to 3,000 metres high in the Himalayas. It is one of many Asian pheasants that are in danger. Grazing herds and fires set by farmers have ruined much of the grass it likes, and it is hunted for food—even inside nature reserves. It has already become extinct in Pakistan and is rare now in most countries.

FOUND IN:
Himalayas

SCIENTIFIC NAME:
Catreus wallichii

MAIN THREATS:
Habitat destruction and hunting

SIZE:
65 cm–1.2 m long

GRASSLAND AND MOUNTAIN ANIMALS

Komodo dragon

Imagine a lizard three metres long and strong enough to kill a deer! The Komodo dragon is a frightening lizard and is sometimes shot because it is known to attack or kill farm animals and even people. But it is also a big tourist attraction. It is specially protected on Komodo and the other few islands where it lives and conservationists hope that the 7,500 lizards that are left will be safe.

FOUND IN:
Indonesia

MAIN THREAT:
Hunting

SCIENTIFIC NAME:
Varanus komodoensis

SIZE:
Up to 3 m long

Przewalski's horse

This wild horse may be an ancestor of the domestic horses we all know, but has not been seen on the plains of Mongolia since 1968. It died out in the wild because of centuries of hunting and heavy grazing of its pastures. Hundreds have been kept in zoos, however, where they have bred well. There are plans to return some into their old Mongolian home.

FOUND IN:
Mongolia

SCIENTIFIC NAME:
Equus przewalskii

MAIN THREATS:
Hunting and habitat disruption

SIZE:
1.8–2 m long

Great bustard

The great bustard lives on open, grassy steppes. But as farming land increases it is gradually being pushed out. Weedkillers, for example, are destroying much of its food and cover. Wandering cattle often disturb it from its nest, and because it does not fly well (at up to 18 kg it is the world's heaviest flying bird), it often collides with hazards like cables.

FOUND IN:
Southern Europe to central Asia

MAIN THREATS:
Habitat destruction and disturbance

SCIENTIFIC NAME:
Otis tarda

SIZE:
75 cm–1 m long

ASIA

Batagur

FOUND IN:
Southeast Asia

SCIENTIFIC NAME:
Batagur baska

MAIN THREATS:
Hunting and habitat destruction

SIZE:
Up to 58 cm long

Batagurs nest on river sandbanks, so it is easy for people to catch them and dig up their eggs for food. In Malaysia, to save the batagur, eggs are taken to hatcheries and young turtles kept safe in pools until they are two years old.

Proboscis monkey

With its large fleshy nose, the proboscis monkey is one of the strangest members of the monkey family. It feeds on leaves and fruit in swamps by the coast and in riverside forests. People also like to live in these places and half of the monkey's habitat has already been cleared away to make room for towns, roads and farms, and to supply wood. The monkey is also hunted for food and for sport.

Baiji

There are only about 300 of these dolphins left in and around China's Yangtze River. Many are killed by accident in boat propellors or in fishing nets. Others cannot find enough to eat because the fish they feed on can no longer live in the polluted waters.

FRESHWATER AND SEA ANIMALS

Mekong catfish

This catfish can grow to more than two metres in length. But full-size fish are rare now in the Mekong River and its tributaries. Each year the adults swim upriver to spawn, and fishermen set traps to catch as many as possible when they return downstream. The fish are not only taken as food: the oil in their bodies is also valuable.

FOUND IN:
Southern China and Southeast Asia

MAIN THREAT:
Overfishing

SCIENTIFIC NAME:
Pangasianodon gigas

SIZE:
Up to 2.5 m long

FOUND IN:
Borneo

MAIN THREATS:
Habitat destruction and hunting

SCIENTIFIC NAME:
Nasalis larvatus

SIZE:
Body 53–76 cm long, tail 56–76 cm

White-eyed river martin

FOUND IN:
Thailand

MAIN THREATS:
Capture and habitat destruction

SCIENTIFIC NAME:
Pseudochelidon sirintarae

SIZE:
Body 15 cm long, tail 9 cm

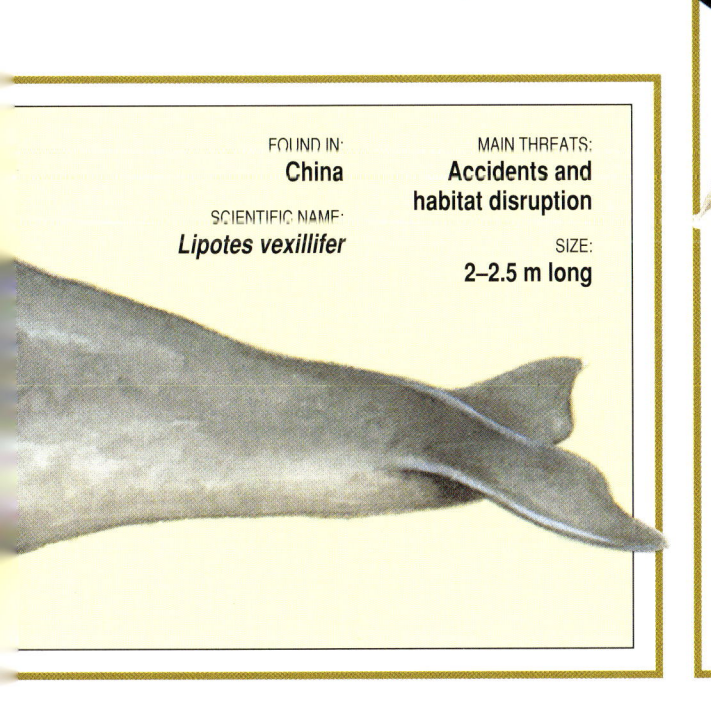

This bird was unknown until 1968 when ten birds were discovered among the large flocks of swallows that roost in the reeds of Lake Boraphet. Since then, few have been found, and they must be close to extinction. There are also fewer swallows on the lake because people trap them and harvest the reeds. These problems probably affect the martins as well.

FOUND IN:
China

MAIN THREATS:
Accidents and habitat disruption

SCIENTIFIC NAME:
Lipotes vexillifer

SIZE:
2–2.5 m long

Australia and New Zealand

The settlers who sailed to Australia and New Zealand brought many problems for the animals that lived there.

Since the late eighteenth century, all sorts of problems have plagued the wildlife of Australia and New Zealand. For hundreds of years, local peoples had left much of the landscape unchanged. But then European settlers began to colonize the land. They laid out farms and ranches where there had once been grasslands and forests. They shot large numbers of wild animals for food and sport, and to protect their livestock.

The biggest threats to native wildlife, however, were the animals and plants that the newcomers brought with them. Sheep and goats grazed pastures so short that they drove out many grass-eating and seed-eating animals. Rats, weasels, cats and foxes found native animals easy to catch. These and other introduced predators have put ten of the seventeen species of birds that live on New Zealand's Chatham Islands in danger of extinction. Foreign grasses have replaced most of New Zealand's natural tussock grass and the rubber vine has infested Australia's rainforests, making the habitat less suitable for native species.

In 1879, the Royal National Park was established near Sydney. Since then, great efforts have been made to protect wildlife. Conservationists are working hard in both countries to preserve habitats and rebuild the populations of vulnerable species.

The Leadbetter's possum lives in hollows in old eucalyptus trees. But if its forest home continues to be destroyed, this already rare animal is in danger of disappearing completely.

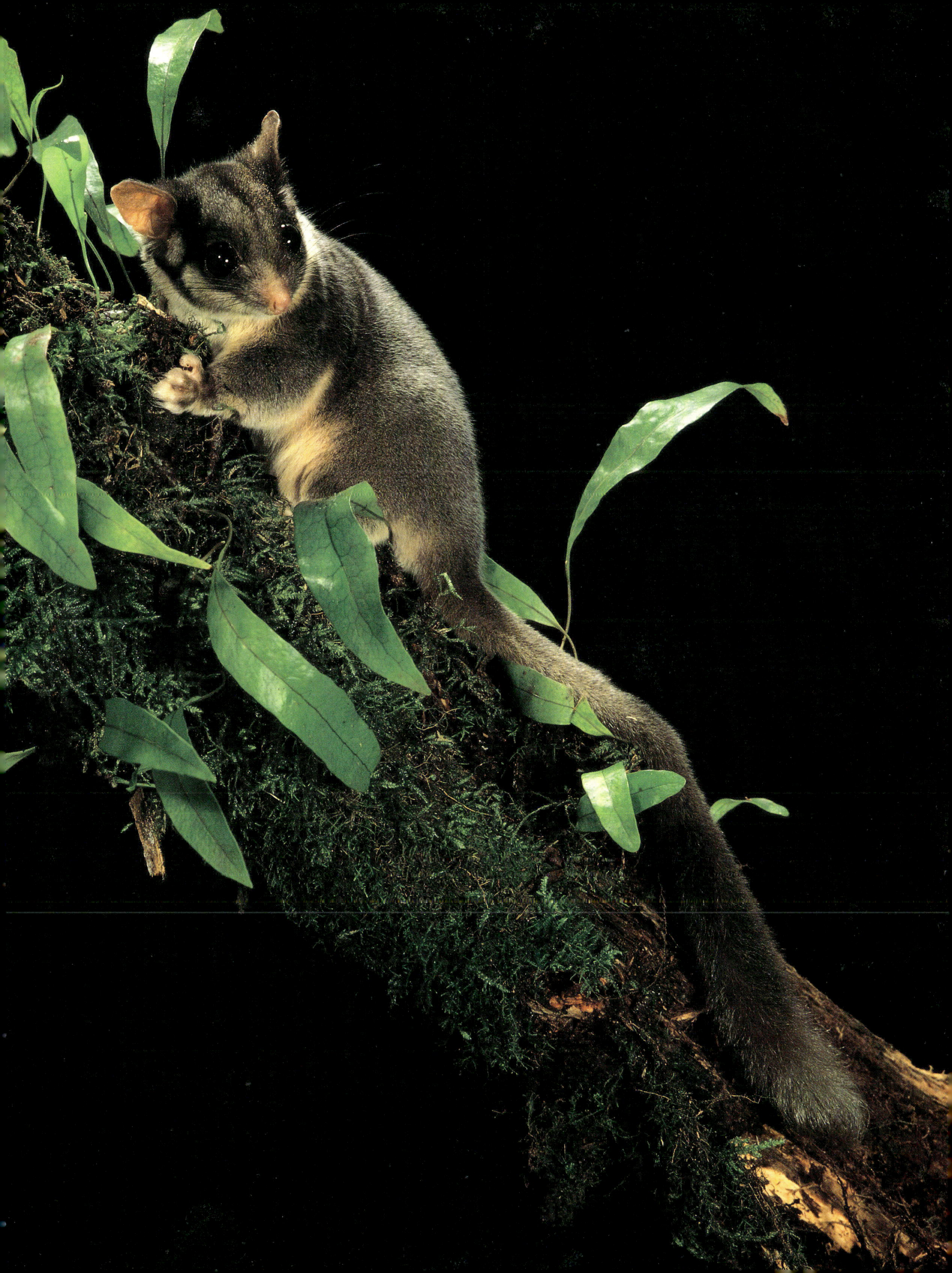

Threatened animals of Australia and New Zealand

① Malleefowl

There is a common threat to the survival of the various endangered animals of Australia and New Zealand. Too often, animals brought from overseas and let loose to roam the land have played a part in the downfall of native creatures. The greater bilby, which was once common in Australia, suffered terribly because of hunting and cattle grazing. But then more problems came from introduced animals. Rabbits took over bilby burrows, foxes attacked it and the bilby is now extinct in many areas. In others it lives only in scattered pockets.

The ring-tailed rock wallaby feeds on the scant plant life in dry, rocky country. It first came under threat from hunters who wanted its handsome fur. Now its main enemies are goats that have invaded its habitat, using up its food supply.

Smaller mammals have also suffered. The numbat has retreated to the southwest corner of Australia. There it uses its strong claws to break into termites' and ants' nests and its long snout to probe inside and eat the occupants. Foxes and cats, as well as fires set to clear land, made life impossible for it in other regions. Birds are also at risk. The malleefowl is famous for building mounds of rotting vegetation where it keeps its eggs warm. Much of its scrubland home has been turned into cropland

⑦ Numbat

⑥ Hochstetter's frog

Australia and New Zealand

② Greater bilby

or is heavily grazed by sheep and rabbits.

Hochstetter's frog lives along forested mountain streams in New Zealand's North Island. It has been wiped out in many areas by rats, and pigs and goats have ruined much of the streamside vegetation. Clearing of New Zealand's forest for farming left little room for the kokako. Only about 1,000 birds remain on North Island and the southern group was thought to be extinct until some were discovered recently on Stewart Island. All the survivors, however, risk attack from rats and cats that raid nests.

Efforts are under way to help most of these animals. One that has already benefited from conservation is the estuarine crocodile. This giant animal is heavily hunted for its hide along the coast of Asia, but because of a strict hunting ban far fewer are killed in northern Australia. It is one of the few places in the world where crocodiles are actually rising in number.

③ Ring-tailed rock wallaby

④ Estuarine crocodile

⑤ Kokako

AUSTRALIA AND NEW ZEALAND

Tuatara

Although it looks like a lizard, the tuatara belongs to a much older group of reptiles, known as the "beaked reptiles". All except the tuatara died out long ago, and when settlers brought new animals to New Zealand the tuatara nearly disappeared as well. Rats, especially, ate so many eggs and young that the tuatara was wiped out on the mainland. Today it survives on about 30 small islands, where constant efforts are made to keep rats out.

FOUND IN:
New Zealand

MAIN THREAT:
Introduced animals

SCIENTIFIC NAME:
Sphenodon punctatus

SIZE:
Up to 65 cm long

Koala

The eucalyptus trees of the koalas' forest home are gradually being destroyed and hunters track the animals for their fur. In 1924 alone, two million skins were exported from Australia. Only a few thousand koalas were left in the wild when laws were made to protect the animals from hunters. Many koalas now live in reserves where their numbers can increase in safety.

FOUND IN:
Eastern Australia

MAIN THREATS:
Habitat destruction and hunting

SCIENTIFIC NAME:
Phascolarctos cinereus

SIZE:
60–85 cm long

Kakapo

FOUND IN:
New Zealand

MAIN THREATS:
Habitat destruction and introduced animals

SCIENTIFIC NAME:
Strigops habroptilus

SIZE:
58–65 cm long

FOREST ANIMALS

Lumholtz's tree kangaroo

FOUND IN:
Northeastern Australia

MAIN THREAT:
Habitat destruction

SCIENTIFIC NAME:
Dendrolagus lumholtzi

SIZE:
Body 48–59 cm long, tail 60–74 cm

Unlike other kangaroos, the tree kangaroo is happy to live high in the forest trees where it eats leaves and fruit. It can even sleep up there, crouched on a thick branch. This species has seen its rainforest home gradually shrink in area, mainly because of logging. But there are now several forest parks and reserves where it should be safe.

Ghost bat

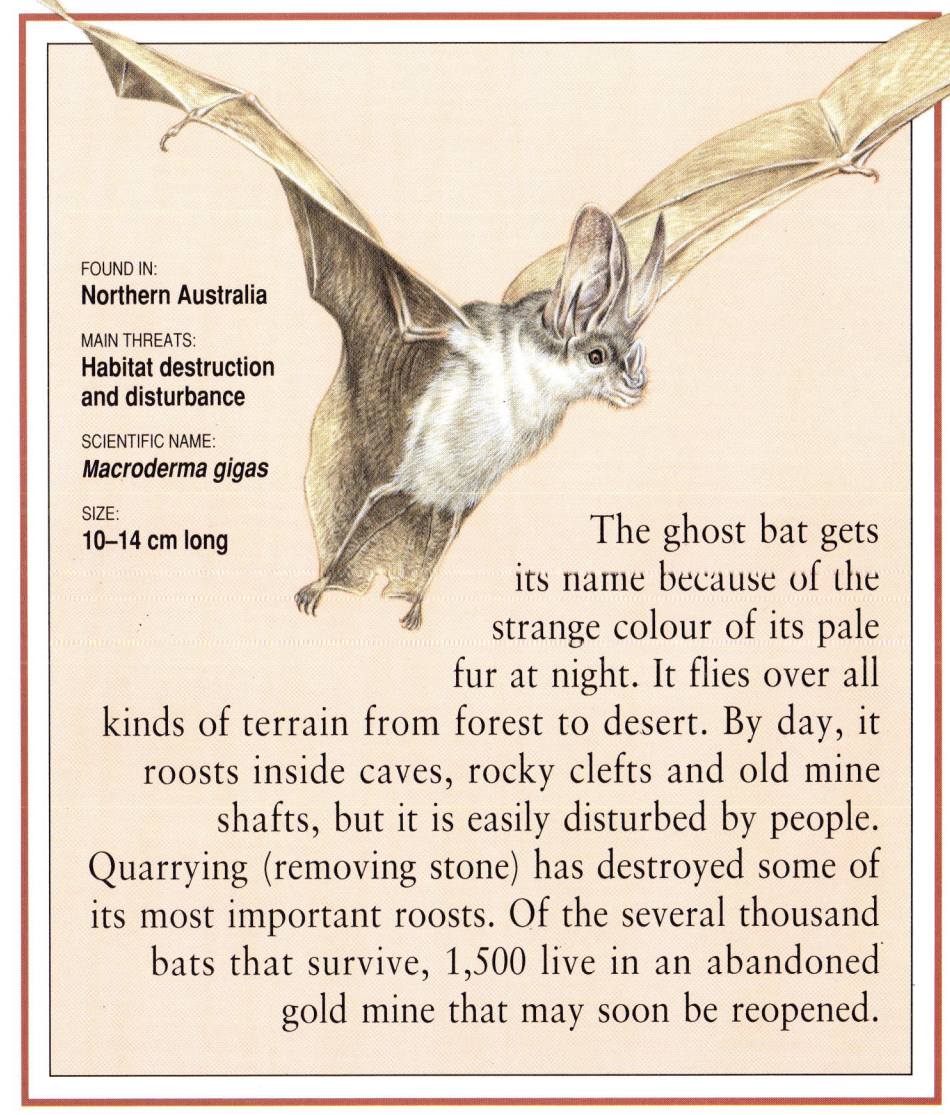

FOUND IN:
Northern Australia

MAIN THREATS:
Habitat destruction and disturbance

SCIENTIFIC NAME:
Macroderma gigas

SIZE:
10–14 cm long

This parrot no longer lives on mainland New Zealand, partly because much of its forest home has been destroyed. Because it lives on the ground and cannot fly, it is easy prey for introduced dogs, cats, rats and ferrets. The 43 birds that are left have been taken to two small islands for safety. It is hoped that they will breed there, but attempts so far have not been successful.

The ghost bat gets its name because of the strange colour of its pale fur at night. It flies over all kinds of terrain from forest to desert. By day, it roosts inside caves, rocky clefts and old mine shafts, but it is easily disturbed by people. Quarrying (removing stone) has destroyed some of its most important roosts. Of the several thousand bats that survive, 1,500 live in an abandoned gold mine that may soon be reopened.

Focus on: Dugong

The waters off northern Australia are the last place of refuge for the dugong. This placid sea mammal used to be seen in warm coastal waters all around the Indian and western Pacific oceans. But its numbers have dwindled everywhere, and along many stretches of coast it is in danger of extinction. Though there are at least several thousand dugongs around Australia, that sometimes appear near the shore in large herds, even this population seems to be getting smaller.

Slow-moving, vulnerable and with a low breeding rate, the dugong simply has trouble surviving in a world ruled by humans. People obstruct the shallows with nets, pollute and damage the sea grasses on which it feeds, and hunt the animal for meat. Only aboriginal peoples are allowed to hunt the dugong in Australia, but some conservationists think that even they kill too many. The best way to save the dugong is probably to create special marine reserves where its habitat is undisturbed.

Browsing in the shallows
The dugong eats little but the leaves and roots of sea grass, which grows in beds in shallow coastal waters. Unfortunately, areas of sea grass are being increasingly ruined by pollution, dredging and burial under sediments.

Innocent victim
Lethal nets designed to keep sharks away from Australian bathing beaches are just one of the many dangers that threaten the dugong. Since 1975 about one dugong a month has been killed by becoming entangled in a net and drowning. On some parts of the coast the dugong is now extremely rare.

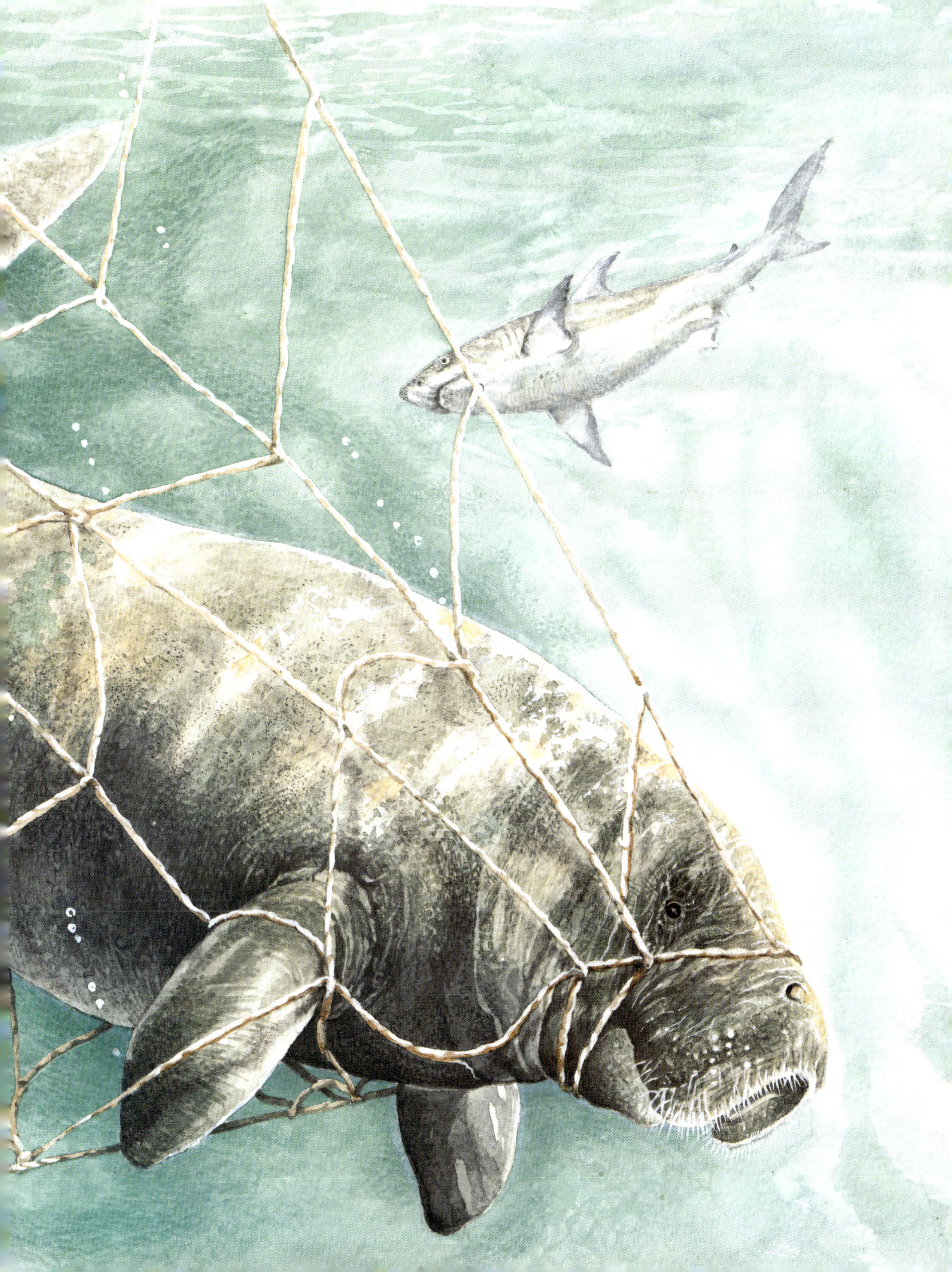

Broad-headed snake

This colourful snake's poison is very strong. It lives near the city of Sydney, and people sometimes kill it out of fear. But the biggest threat is that people take the rocks under which it shelters by day to decorate their gardens: in some places it no longer has anywhere to hide.

FOUND IN:
Southeastern Australia

MAIN THREAT:
Habitat disruption

SCIENTIFIC NAME:
Hoplocephalus bungaroides

SIZE:
Up to 60 cm long

Stick-nest rat

This rat has disappeared from the mainland. Many of the places where it lived have been made into farmland. Cattle trampled its nests, farm animals chewed the juicy plants it eats and it was attacked by cats and foxes. The rat survives only on Franklin Island, and if its enemies reach the island, it will probably become extinct.

FOUND IN:
Southern Australia

MAIN THREATS:
Habitat destruction and introduced animals

SCIENTIFIC NAME:
Leporillus conditor

SIZE:
Body 17–26 cm long, tail 15–18 cm

Gouldian finch

FOUND IN:
Northern Australia

MAIN THREATS:
Capture and disease

SCIENTIFIC NAME:
Chloebia gouldiae

SIZE:
13–14 cm long

Flocks of this beautiful finch busily forage for grass seeds in the hottest weather. Sadly, fewer and fewer birds now live in the wild. This may be because many were trapped for sale as cage birds and died on the way to the pet shops. But scientists have now found that many finches are infested with a dangerous parasite. This disease may have spread to wild flocks from escaped caged birds.

GRASSLAND AND SCRUBLAND ANIMALS

Takahe

FOUND IN:
New Zealand

MAIN THREAT:
Introduced animals

SCIENTIFIC NAME:
Porphyrio mantelli

SIZE:
60–64 cm long

New Zealanders thought the flightless, seed-eating takahe was extinct, but in 1948 some birds were rediscovered on South Island. With careful conservation, their numbers have risen there to about 260, and some birds that were raised in captivity have been set free. It is important to keep the takahes' two main enemies at bay—stoats, which attack them, and red deer, which eat their food.

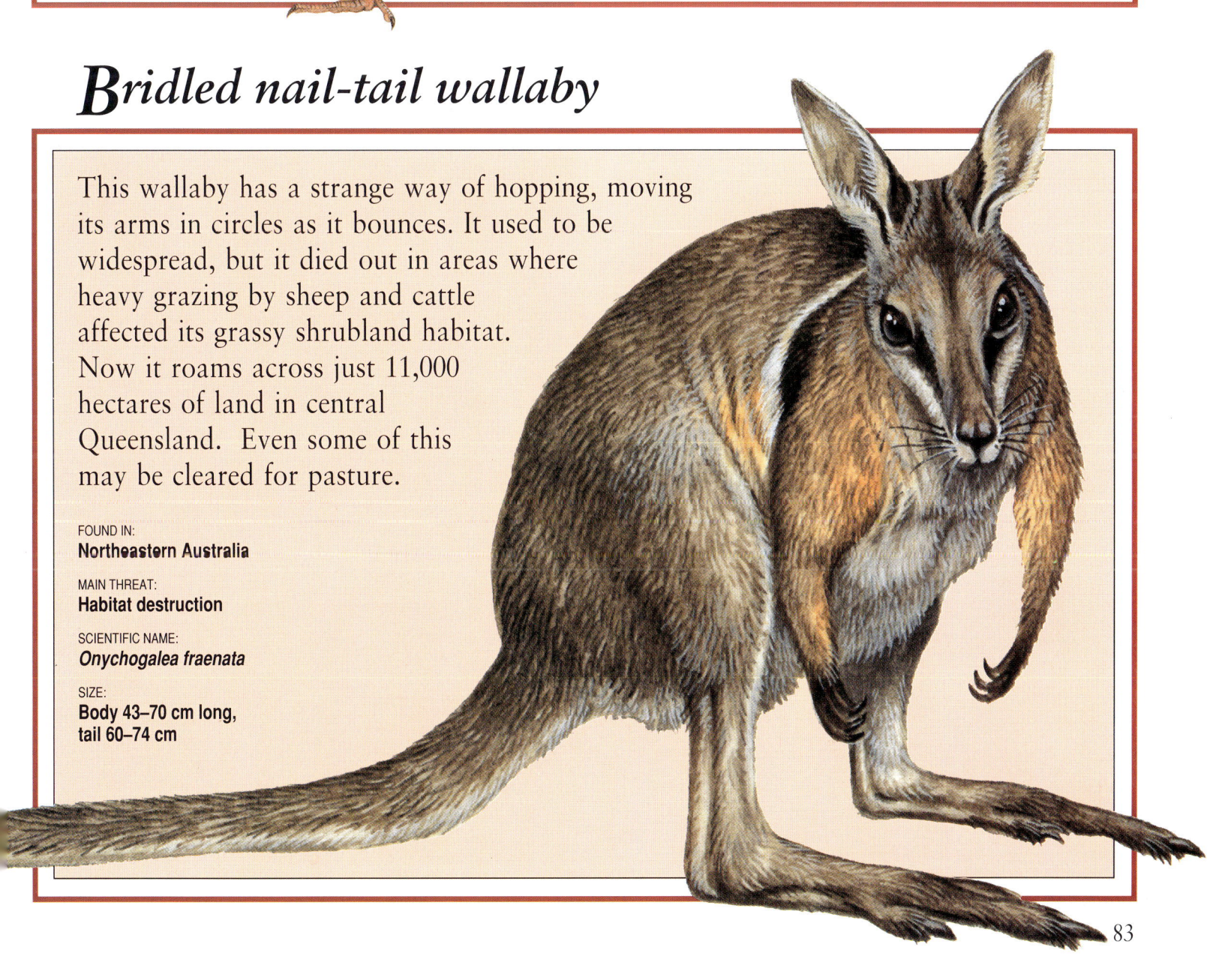

Bridled nail-tail wallaby

This wallaby has a strange way of hopping, moving its arms in circles as it bounces. It used to be widespread, but it died out in areas where heavy grazing by sheep and cattle affected its grassy shrubland habitat. Now it roams across just 11,000 hectares of land in central Queensland. Even some of this may be cleared for pasture.

FOUND IN:
Northeastern Australia

MAIN THREAT:
Habitat destruction

SCIENTIFIC NAME:
Onychogalea fraenata

SIZE:
Body 43–70 cm long, tail 60–74 cm

Oceanic islands

Islands can be dangerous places for wildlife, but their small size may make them ideal conservation areas.

The small, remote islands that lie far out in the oceans are home to many endangered animals. Because space is in short supply, these animals exist in very small populations, and most do not live anywhere else. This puts each species at risk. A volcanic eruption or a fierce storm could wipe out the entire population overnight.

Usually, however, the changes caused by people are the greatest threat. As the human population of the islands grows, more and more natural habitats disappear. The goats, pigs, sheep and cattle that people keep eat away native vegetation. Few island plants have stinging hairs, prickles or a bitter taste to deter large plant eaters.

Other introduced animals kill wildlife directly. Most native island creatures are not used to such enemies as rats, cats and mongooses, and they have few defences. Many of the birds, for example, cannot even fly. Some do not recognize danger. The now extinct dodo, which used to live on the island of Mauritius in the Indian Ocean, was so tame that sailors could walk up and club it to death for food.

Conservation on oceanic islands has been slow to start, but already there are hopeful signs. Strict protection in the Galapagos Islands is helping many unique species. And Cousin Island in the Seychelles was set aside for conservation in 1968. Since then the island's population of the rare Seychelles brush warbler has already greatly increased.

Pollution and attacks from dogs and cats could greatly harm the marine iguana, which lives on rocky shores in the Galapagos Islands. Conservationists work hard to keep threats like these at bay.

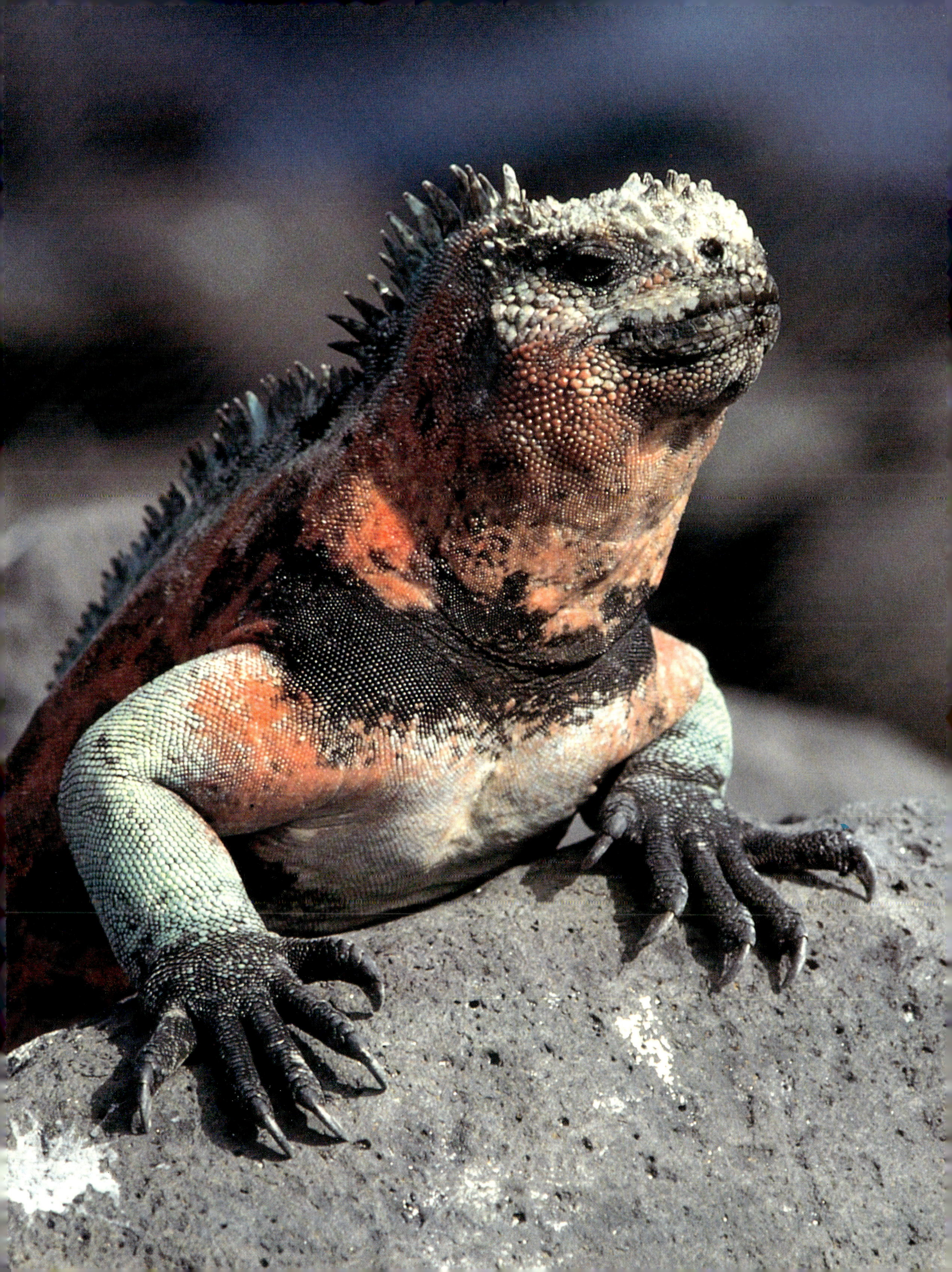

Threatened Animals of Oceanic Islands

The story of Hawaii shows us how vulnerable island wildlife can be. Many Hawaiian animals began to decline more than 1,000 years ago when Polynesian settlers started to hunt and farm on the islands and introduced rats there. By the time Europeans arrived, one half of its bird species had been driven to extinction. Several more have since followed. The akiapolaau is one of the survivors, but only just. This bird, which uses its extraordinary upper bill to winkle insects out of tree bark, now lives only in small patches of old forest invaded by goats, sheep and pigs.

Nature on other, smaller islands is just as fragile. On Christmas Island, mining has destroyed a large part of the forest where the Abbott's booby nests. Its population has fallen to just 1,500 pairs. The tiny 2.5 cm Seychelles frog has lost most of its mountain forest home to farming and is harmed by introduced animals including exotic frogs that take over its habitat.

Cats exterminated the Ascension frigatebird on Ascension Island. Now this seabird nests only on Boatswainbird Island, a rocky islet just off shore. If cats arrived there it would quickly die out. The same fate would befall the Inaccessible Island rail if cats or rats ever reached its remote island home. At present there are about 4,000 of these rails, but they are tiny birds, unable to fly and easy prey for any invading enemy.

Sea creatures are usually less vulnerable because they are more widespread and numerous, but not all are safe. The giant clam, which can weigh more than

① Seychelles frog

⑦ Galapagos giant tortoise

⑥ Inaccessible Island rail

Oceanic Islands

② Abbott's booby

200 kg, lives around islands in the western Pacific. People have taken so many clams for their meat and their impressive shells that the species has disappeared from some coasts.

Efforts are under way to conserve the Galapagos giant tortoise. It has suffered from hunting, habitat destruction and egg-stealing predators, but is being helped by strict protection from introduced animals and captive breeding.

③ Giant clam

④ Ascension frigatebird

⑤ Akiapolaau

87

OCEANIC ISLANDS

Fijian banded iguana

This long-tailed lizard is a good tree climber, with long toes to give it a firm grip. But iguanas can no longer hide from their enemies because trees on its islands are being burned and felled, and goats browse heavily on the remaining plants. Its worst enemy is the mongoose which eats both eggs and young. Wherever the mongoose has been released, the iguana is very rare.

FOUND IN:
Fiji and Tonga (Pacific Ocean)

MAIN THREATS:
Introduced animals and habitat destruction

SCIENTIFIC NAME:
Brachylophus fasciatus

SIZE:
Up to 90 cm long

Kauai o-o

FOUND IN:
Hawaii (Pacific Ocean)

MAIN THREATS:
Habitat destruction and introduced animals

SCIENTIFIC NAME:
Moho braccatus

SIZE:
19–21 cm long

One hundred years ago, this darting, insect-eating bird was common all over Kauai island in Hawaii. But much of its rainforest home was destroyed and black rats invaded the island. The rats raided nests and killed adults, nearly causing the o-o to become extinct. A small group of birds was discovered in 1960, but it was too late to save the o-o. In 1989, only one solitary male could be found.

Tooth-billed pigeon

This pigeon spends most of its time on the ground, where it eats leaves, seeds and berries. It has a hooked bill similar to that of the dodo and, like that extinct island bird, the tooth-billed pigeon has been hunted for its meat. It has also suffered from the release of harmful animals such as cats and rats that attack the bird, and pigs that ruin its nests.

FOUND IN:
Western Samoa (Pacific Ocean)

MAIN THREATS:
Hunting and introduced animals

SCIENTIFIC NAME:
Didunculus strigirostris

SIZE:
32–34 cm long

Mauritius kestrel

FOUND IN:
Mauritius (Indian Ocean)

MAIN THREAT:
Habitat destruction

SCIENTIFIC NAME:
Falco punctatus

SIZE:
28–33 cm long

The Mauritius kestrel, which hunts in dense forest for lizards and small birds, has been at the brink of extinction. In 1986, there were just six wild kestrels left on the island in untouched forest on mountain slopes. But many more were being raised in cages and have since been set free. Now the wild population stands at nearly 200.

Rodrigues flying fox

In 1974, when there were fewer than 80 alive, this flying fox was probably the rarest bat in the world. It eats fruit and needs plenty of trees so it can find food all year round, but only a tiny part of Rodrigues is still forested. The bats' roosting site is now protected, new fruit trees have been planted and numbers have risen to about 400. But the threat of freak weather remains—in 1979 half the colony died after fierce winds hit the island.

FOUND IN:
Rodrigues (Indian Ocean)

MAIN THREATS:
Habitat destruction and natural disaster

SCIENTIFIC NAME:
Pteropus rodricensis

SIZE:
17–20 cm long

Focus on: Hawaiian goose

At the end of the eighteenth century, there may have been 25,000 Hawaiian geese. But settlers came to Hawaii and turned the land into farms and ranches. They introduced grazing animals and exotic predators and they hunted the birds for meat. The geese seemed to be doomed. One of their worst enemies was the mongoose, which was released on the islands to kill rats in sugar plantations but soon started killing the native animals. By 1947, only about 30 wild geese remained.

But all was not lost. Special captive-breeding projects for the geese were started at Pohakuloa in Hawaii and at Slimbridge in England. Eventually there were enough captive birds to start releasing them into the wild. Today there are up to 500 geese flying free on the high, open slopes of the islands of Hawaii, Kauai and Maui. However, the future of the Hawaiian goose, also known as the nene, is still at risk. Conservationists have tried to keep introduced animals away (sometimes by trapping them), but the geese that have been released still have not been able to raise many young.

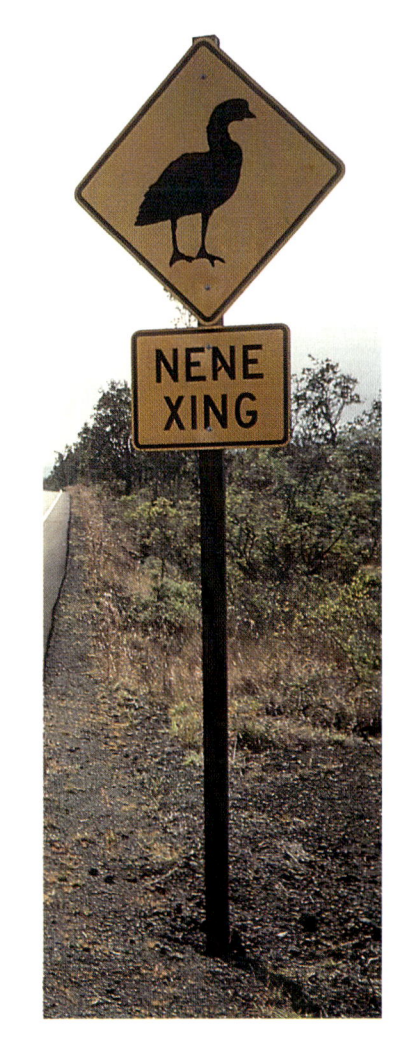

Help at hand
Numbers of Hawaiian geese have increased thanks to an international rescue effort. At the Slimbridge breeding centre in England (above) as well as in Hawaii, hundreds of geese have been reared in safety since the 1950s. Many have now been released back into the wild. But in their native Hawaii busy roads can be another danger (left).

Deadly intruder
Nesting Hawaiian geese have little defence against an attacking mongoose. This swift-moving hunter can easily steal eggs and chicks and can even kill an adult goose if it is moulting and unable to fly.

91

OCEANIC ISLANDS

St. Helena earwig

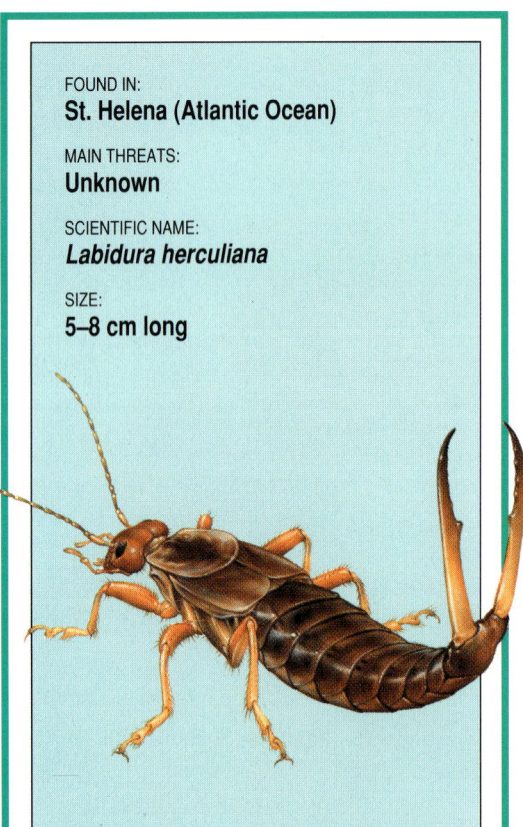

FOUND IN:
St. Helena (Atlantic Ocean)
MAIN THREATS:
Unknown
SCIENTIFIC NAME:
Labidura herculiana
SIZE:
5–8 cm long

In 1798 a giant eight-centimetre earwig was spotted on the remote island of St. Helena, but it was not until 1965 that the insect was found again. Little is known about the insect but it seems to live only in a tiny, barren area in the northeast of the island. The earwig has long forceps on its head but no wings. It lives in burrows and comes out at night—but only in the rainy season.

Hawaiian hawk

In 1968 there were no more than a few hundred of these hawks left on Hawaii. Many had been killed as pests by farmers and sometimes shot for sport. Now hunting is against the law and the hawk population is recovering, although the birds are still suffering from the loss of much of their forest home. There may now be as many as 2,000 Hawaiian hawks.

FOUND IN:
Hawaii (Pacific Ocean)
MAIN THREATS:
Hunting and habitat destruction
SCIENTIFIC NAME:
Buteo solitarius
SIZE:
41–46 cm long

Land iguana

The land iguana chews plants, including spiny cacti, and has a strong body for digging burrows in the earth. In the past, it was hunted for sport and for its

SCRUBLAND AND COASTAL ANIMALS

Flightless cormorant

Robber crab

FOUND IN:
Galapagos (Pacific Ocean)

MAIN THREATS:
Accidents and introduced animals

SCIENTIFIC NAME:
Nannopterum harrisi

SIZE:
87–90 cm long

With its small, ragged wings this cormorant is not able to fly, but up until now it has not needed to. It lives on rocky coasts and simply dives into the water to catch octopus and other seafood when it is hungry. But the cormorants might not be safe in the future. Local fishermen may soon be allowed to use nets, which could easily entangle the birds, and introduced dogs could damage the nesting colonies.

This big land crab lives under rocks or in burrows on tropical islands. Islanders love to eat the crab and it has been hunted so heavily that it has disappeared completely from Mauritius. Now some of the other islands have introduced laws to protect the robber crab from hunters.

flesh (especially its tail). This, along with attacks on its young by dogs, cats and rats, led to its disappearance from many Galapagos islands. On the islands where it survives, goats are its main enemy – they eat the plant life, leaving little for the iguana.

FOUND IN:
Galapagos (Pacific Ocean)

MAIN THREATS:
Hunting and introduced animals

SCIENTIFIC NAME:
Conolophus subcristatus

SIZE:
Up to 1.1 m long

FOUND IN:
Indian Ocean and Pacific Ocean islands

SCIENTIFIC NAME:
Birgus latro

MAIN THREAT:
Hunting

SIZE:
Up to 1 m legspan

93

RESOURCE LIST

Environmental and conservation organizations, some of which are listed below, are useful sources of information about endangered species. These organizations have limited funds and materials, and most prefer written requests for information. When writing, please include self-addressed stamped envelopes and be patient while waiting for a response.

ORGANIZATIONS FOR THE CONSERVATION OF PARTICULAR SPECIES

Barn Owl Trust
Waterleat, Ashburton, Devon TQ13 7H
0364 53026
A charity dedicated to conserving the barn owl and its natural habitat in the UK. Produces a full range of leaflets available on request. "Feedback" newsletter received on donations over £5.

Bat Conservation Trust
The London Ecology Centre, 45 Shelton Street, London WC2H 9HJ.   071 240 0933
Britain's only organization devoted solely to the conservation of bats. Junior and family membership available. Produces a termly newsletter, "The Young Batworker".

British Butterfly Conservation Society
PO Box 222, Dedham, Colchester, Essex CO7 6EY
0509 412 870
Largest society in the world devoted to the study of butterflies. Surveys populations in certain habitats and lobbies for the conservation of areas. Junior membership available.

National Federation of Badger Groups
7 London Road, Tetbury, Gloucestershire
GL8 8JQ.   0666 503 419
An umbrella organization that coordinates a number of groups throughout the country for the protection, welfare and conservation of badgers.

Otter Trust
Earsham near Bungay, Suffolk NR35 2AF
0986 893470
Promotes the conservation of otters and wetland habitats throughout the world. Maintains a collection of otters in semi-natural conditions for research and education. Junior membership available. HQ open daily for visitors and produces a newsletter, "Otter Tracks".

Project: Save the Nene
The Wildfowl & Wetlands Trust, Slimbridge, Gloucestershire GL2 7BT
Special project to rescue the nene (Hawaiian goose) from extinction. Birds are being bred in captivity for return to the wild. Information available on request.

Whale and Dolphin Conservation Society
19a James Street West, Bath, Avon BA1 2BT
0225 334511
Promotes public awareness of the plight of whales and dolphins. Also organizes the "Adopt a Whale" scheme. Youth membership available for under 18s, produces a magazine, "Sonar", twice a year.

GENERAL ORGANIZATIONS

Amateur Entomologists Society
22 Salisbury Road, Feltham, Middlesex
TW13 5DP.   081 890 3584
Society for the study of insects. Primarily for amateurs, but with a panel of experts to help with identification. Also has a section for young people. Produces a bi-monthly magazine and publishes books on methods of entomology.

Animal Action Club
RSPCA, Causeway, Horsham, West Sussex
RH12 1HG.   0402 264181
Junior club of the RSPCA for the under 17s. Provides information regarding campaigns and also organizes Animal Treks. Produces a magazine, "Animal World", six times a year.

Born Free Foundation
Coldharbour, Dorking, Surrey RH5 6HA
0306 712 091
An animal welfare charity that coordinates the work of Zoo Check, ELEFRIENDS, Into the Blue, The Great Ape Escape and Operation Wolf. Members are invited to join in unique annual "Wildlife Workshops". Offers children's rates and produces a newsletter.

British Trust for Ornithology
The Nunnery, Thetford, Norfolk IP24 2PU
0842 750050
A working partnership of amateur birdwatchers and professional research staff that encourages the serious study of British wild birds and advises on their conservation. Produces a regular bulletin.

Fauna and Flora Preservation Society
1 Kensington Gore, London SW7 2AR
071 823 8899
Promotes the conservation of wildlife throughout the world. Offers family and junior membership and produces a quarterly magazine.

Friends of the Earth
(England, Wales and Northern Ireland)
26-28 Underwood Street, London N1 7JQ
071 490 1555
(Scotland)
70-72 Newhaven Road, Edinburgh EH6 5QG
031 554 9977
Through public education and direct governmental lobbying, this organization works to promote policy changes and affect public opinion regarding environmental issues.

Go Wild Club
WWF UK, PO BOX 101, Wetherby, Yorkshire
LS23 6EE.   0937 541 542
Junior branch of the WWF for members aged 7 to 15. Membership includes a fact file containing information on the environment. Produces a magazine four times a year.

Greenpeace
Canonbury Villas, London N1 2PN.   071 354 5100
Uses direct non-violent action and lobbying to campaign against abuse of the environment.

Marine Conservancy Council
9 Gloucester Road, Ross-on-Wye, Herefordshire
HR9 5BU.   0989 66017
Britain's only environment group concerned solely with the marine environment. Campaigns to protect the wildlife of coastal and offshore waters.

Media Natura
21 Tower Street, London WC2 9NS.   071 240 4936
Charity founded to bring an understanding of the media to environment and aid groups. Offers support regarding the full range of communications from television production to design.

People's Trust for Endangered Species
Hamble House, Meadrow, Godalming, Surrey GU7 3JX.   0483 424848
Funds and promotes projects whose results and research benefit endangered animals in their natural habitation. Produces an annual newsletter.

Rainforest Foundation
2 Ingate Place, Battersea, London SW8 3NS
071 498 7603
Promotes worldwide awareness of the need to conserve the tropical forests and support the indigenous people in their efforts to conserve their land. Family and junior membership available. Produces a bi-monthly journal.

Watch Trust for Environmental Education
RSNC, The Green, Witham Park, Waterside South, Lincoln LN2 2NR.   0552 544400
Junior section of the Royal Society for Nature Conservation. Encourages children to take an active role in protecting the environment. Adults may become associate members, helpers or group leaders. Produces a magazine three times a year as well as project packs, kits and publications.

Young Ornithologists Club
RSPB, The Lodge, Sandy, Bedfordshire SG19 2DL
0767 680551
World's largest club for young people interested in birds and wildlife. Organizes surveys and explorer days, as well as running 115 nature reserves. Offers group membership for schools and produces a bi-monthly magazine as well as a quarterly newsletter for older members.

Young People's Trust for the Environment and Nature Conservation
95 Woodbridge Road, Guildford, Surrey GU1 4PY
0483 39600
Offers an education and information service, in particular a free lecture service aimed at schools. Also organizes field trips and summer holidays for 9 to 16 year olds.

INDEX

A
addax 48–49
akiapolaau 87
alligator, American 27
Amazon river dolphin (boto) 39
anemone, starlet sea 54
armadillo, giant 33
auk, great 11
aye-aye 45

B
baiji (Chinese river dolphin) 72–73
barbet, toucan 32
bat
   ghost 79
   greater horseshoe 56
batagur (river terrapin) 72
bear
   grizzly 15
   spectacled 36
bilby, greater 76–77
bird of paradise, ribbon-tailed 67
bison
   American 15, 18
   European 56–57
bontebok 42–43
booby, Abbott's 86–87
boto (Amazon river dolphin) 39
buffalo 16
bustard, great 71
butterfly
   fluminense swallowtail 37
   large copper 52–53
   Queen Alexandra's birdwing 67

C
caiman
   broad-nosed 30–31
   spectacled 38–39
cat, wild 55
catfish, Mekong 73
chimpanzee 45
clam, giant 87
coelacanth 51
conch, queen 26
condor, Californian 19
cormorant, flightless 93
corncrake 56
cougar 18–19
coypu 54
crab, robber 93
crane
   Siberian white 64–65
   whooping 26–27
crocodile
   estuarine 76–77
   Nile 42–43
   West African dwarf 50
curlew, eskimo 25

D
deer, pampas 28, 36–37
desman, Russian 54
dodo 11, 84, 89
dog, hunting 49
dolphin
   baiji (Chinese river dolphin) 72–73
   boto (Amazon river dolphin) 39
dove, blue-headed quail 18–19
dugong 80–81

E
eagle
   bald 15, 16
   Madagascar fish 50
   Philippine 10–11
earwig, St. Helena 92
elephant
   African 46–47
   Asian 62

F
ferret, black-footed 24
finch, Gouldian 82
flying fox, Rodrigues 88–89
frigatebird, Ascension 86–87
frog
   Hochstetter's 76–77
   Seychelles 86–87

G
gibbon, pileated 66
goose, Hawaiian (nene) 90–91
gorilla, mountain 40
grebe, hooded 30–31

H
hawk, Hawaiian 92
hippopotamus, pygmy 44–45
hobby 54
hornbill, helmeted 66
horse, Przewalski's 70–71
hutia, Ingraham's 21
hyena, brown 42–43

I
ibis, hermit 48
iguana
   Fijian banded 88
   land 92–93
   marine 84–85
   rhinoceros 25
indri 42–43

J
jaguar 30

K
kakapo 78–79
kangaroo, Lumholtz's tree 79
kauai o-o 88
kestrel, Mauritius 89
kite, red 57
koala 78
kokako 77
komodo dragon 71

L
leech, medicinal 60
lemur
   indri 42–43
   ruffed 44
leopard, snow 70
lizard, Komodo dragon 71

M
macaque, Barbary 42
macaw
   hyacinth 34–35
   indigo 30–31
malleefowl 76
manatee, West Indian 19
martin, white-eyed river 73
mongoose 90–91
monkey
   Allen's swamp 51
   proboscis 72–73
   white uakari 30–31
   woolly spider 32
muskrat 54

N
nene (Hawaiian goose) 90–91
numbat 76

O
olm 61
onager 64–65
orangutan 68–69
oryx, Arabian 13, 62–63
otter, European 58–59
owl
   barn 54–55
   northern spotted 13

P
panda, giant 64–65
peacock, Congo 44
peccary, chaco 30–31
pelican, Dalmatian 60
pheasant, cheer 70
pigeon
   passenger 16
   tooth-billed 89
   Victoria-crowned 64–65
pirarucu 39
possum, Leadbetter's 74–75
pronghorn 24–25
python, Indian 64–65

Q
quagga 11
quetzal, resplendent 21

R
rabbit, volcano 18
rail, Inaccessible Island 86–87
rat, stick-nest 82
rhinoceros
   black 42–43
   Sumatran 66–67
rockfowl, white-necked 42

95

S

salamander, olm 61
screamer, northern 38
sea cow, steller's 11
seal, Mediterranean monk 60–61
sheep, bighorn 15
snake
 broad-headed 82
 Indian python 64–65
solenodon, Cuban 20
spatuletail, marvellous 32–33
spider, red-kneed tarantula 24–25
sturgeon, common 60–61

T

takahe 83
tamarin
 emperor 33
 golden lion 28–29
tapir, Malayan 64–65
tarantula, red-kneed 24–25
terrapin, river (batagur) 72
tiger 64–65
tortoise
 chaco 37
 Galapagos giant 86
 pancake 48
 spur-thighed 56–57
tuatara 78

turtle
 Arrau river (South American river) 38
 Central American river 19
 Kemp's ridley 22–23
 loggerhead 54–55

U

uakari, white 30–31

V

vicuna 30–31

W

wallaby
 bridled nail-tail 83
 ring-tailed rock 76–77
warbler, Seychelles brush 84
whale
 bowhead 55
 grey 26–27
woodpecker, ivory-billed 20–21

Z

zebra, Grevy's 49

ACKNOWLEDGEMENTS

ILLUSTRATION CREDITS

Animal illustrations by:
Graham Allen, Alan Male, Colin Newman, Michael Woods

and Norman Arlott, Dianne Breeze, Malcolm Ellis, Robert Gillmor, Vana Haggerty, Peter Hayman, Steve Kirk, Norman Lacey, Denys Ovenden, Myke Taylor, Dick Twinney, Owen Williams, Ken Wood

Maps:
Peter Ferris

Focus spreads:
Priscilla Barret: 46–47, 58–59, 68–69, 80–81, 90–91
Tudor Humphries: 22–23, 34–35

PHOTOGRAPHIC CREDITS

10 P. Morris/Ardea; 12 S. Morgan/Greenpeace; 13 Mark N. Boulton/Bruce Coleman; 16–17 Jim Simmen/ ZEFA-Allstock; 22–23 Matt Bradley/Tom Stack & Associates; 28–29 E.A. Janes/NHPA; 34 top Jany Sauvenet/ NHPA; 34 bottom Martin Wright/Still Pictures; 40–41 K. and K. Ammann/Planet Earth Pictures; 46 Peter Johnson/ NHPA; 47 Rob Hadley/Impact Photos; 52–53 Dennis Green/Bruce Coleman; 59 Geoff du Feu/Planet Earth Pictures; 62–63 Mark N. Boulton/Bruce Coleman; 69 top John Mason/Ardea; 69 bottom Richard Matthews/Planet Earth Pictures; 74–75 Jean-Paul Ferrero/Ardea; 80 D. Parer and E. Parer-Cook/Auscape International; 84–85 François Gohier/Ardea; 90 The Wildfowl and Wetlands Trust, Slimbridge; 90–91 Philippa Stott/NHPA.

The Publishers would also like to thank Jeff Black of The Wildfowl and Wetlands Trust, Slimbridge, UK for help and advice on the Hawaiian goose; Sara O'Grady for providing information on the dugong; and Lindsay McTeague, Tim Probart, Anne Yelland and Clare Truscott for their invaluable editorial assistance.